Samuel Sharpe, Joseph Bonomi

The Alabaster Sarcophagus of Oimeneptah I. - King of Egypt

Now in Sir John Soane's Museum, Lincoln's Inn Fields

Samuel Sharpe, Joseph Bonomi

The Alabaster Sarcophagus of Oimeneptah I. - King of Egypt
Now in Sir John Soane's Museum, Lincoln's Inn Fields

ISBN/EAN: 9783337236991

Printed in Europe, USA, Canada, Australia, Japan

Cover: Foto ©ninafisch / pixelio.de

More available books at **www.hansebooks.com**

THE ALABASTER SARCOPHAGUS

OF

OIMENEPTHAH I., KING OF EGYPT.

NOW IN

SIR JOHN SOANE'S MUSEUM, LINCOLN'S INN FIELDS.

DRAWN BY JOSEPH BONOMI,

AND DESCRIBED BY SAMUEL SHARPE.

LONDON:
LONGMAN, GREEN, LONGMAN, ROBERTS, AND GREEN.
1864.

LONDON
PRINTED BY SPOTTISWOODE AND CO., NEW-STREET SQUARE
AND PARLIAMENT STREET

TO THE MEMORY OF

GIOVANNI BATTISTA BELZONI,

WHO DISENTOMBED THIS SCULPTURED MONUMENT

AND OF

SIR JOHN SOANE,

WHO BOUGHT IT AND GAVE IT TO

THE BRITISH NATION.

CONTENTS.

	PAGE
The Tomb	1
On the King's Names	1
.. the Age of the Sarcophagus	6
.. the Temple of Errebek	8
.. the Hall of Columns at Karnak	9
.. the Buildings at Abydos	10
.. the Flaminian Obelisk at Rome	11
.. the Antiquities in the British Museum	12
.. the Alabaster Sarcophagus	14
Description of the Plates:	
Plate 1	20
Plates 2 to 8—The outside	21
Plates 2 and 3—First picture	22
Plates 3 and 4—Second picture	23
Plates 4 and 5—Third picture	24
Plates 5, 6, and 7—Fourth picture	25
Plates 7 and 8—Fifth picture	26
Plates 9 and 10—Sixth picture	27
Plates 10 and 11—Seventh picture	28
Plates 12 and 13—Eighth picture	29
Plates 13, 14, and 15—Ninth picture	31
Plate 15—Tenth picture	31
Plates 16 and 17—The Bottom of the Chest	34
Plate 18—Broken Pieces of the Right Side of the Lid	36
Plate 19—Broken Pieces of the Left Side of the Lid, and the King's various Names	38
Appendix: Tabular View of Kings' Names	40

LIST OF THE WOODCUTS.

Neith, the Goddess of Heaven, in the sacred tree, pouring the water of life and knowledge into the mouths of a man and of his soul in the form of a bird with human head and hands. From a tablet in the British Museum . . . . TITLE-PAGE.

	PAGE
Fig. 1. Plan and Section of the tomb, from Llereau's *Panorame d'Egypte*	2
2. The king embracing the god Osiris	3
3. The Abyssinian Fenek, and the hieroglyphic copied from it	5
4. Plan of the Temple of Errebek. Lepsius	8
5. View of the ruined portico. Hereau	9
6. Plan of the Temple of Karnak. Lepsius	10
7. View in the Hall of Columns at Karnak. Owen Jones	11
8. Column, with a full-blown Papyrus capital	11
9. „ „ „ Papyrus bud capital	11
10. Four gods of the dead on Canobic jars	21
11. The sun with rays in the daytime, and the sun held up by the ocean in the night	33
12. The sculptor's canon ; or, the proportions of the human figure	35
Chronological series of kings' names	44

THE SARCOPHAGUS OF OIMENEPTHAH I.

ON THE TOMB.

IN October, 1815, the enterprising traveller Belzoni was in Thebes, with a party of labourers in his service exploring the ruins, and more particularly searching for tombs on the western bank of the Nile. On the 16th of the month, he directed his men to open the earth at the foot of one of the hills in the Biban el Molook, or Valley of Kings' Tombs, in the very bed of a watercourse, down which, when the rain falls, a torrent of water rushes towards the Nile. Their labours were soon rewarded by their finding in this unlikely spot that the ground had been before opened. They continued their work on the 17th and 18th; and on the latter day, a day memorable in the history of Egyptian discoveries, they came upon the entrance of an unusually important tomb eighteen feet below the surface of the ground. Having made an opening through the rubbish, and descended the first staircase, our discoverer reached the first corridor or passage, thirty-six feet long.

A second staircase of twenty-three feet and a second sculptured corridor of thirty-seven feet led into a small room, marked A in our plan and section, Fig. 1. This was about thirteen feet square. It was also a well or pit thirty feet deep, crossing the footpath of an intruder into the tomb, so as to bar his further progress, and also formed to catch any water that might drain into the tomb from the surface of the earth.

On the opposite side of this pit was a small opening of less than a yard square, through which some former intruder had entered; and in the pit were the two rope ladders by the help of which he had passed it, first descending to the bottom, and then ascending on the other side.

This small opening had been broken through the wall by which the entrance to the rooms beyond had been carefully closed after the body had been placed in what was meant for its last resting-place.

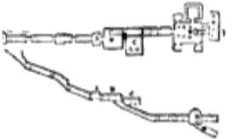

Fig. 1. Plan and Section of the Tomb.

On passing this pit or well, the discoverer entered the first grand hall marked a in our plan and section. This is about twenty-six feet square, and its roof is upheld by four pillars. Beyond this is a second hall, of about the same size, marked c. From this there was no outlet. Returning, therefore, into the first hall, he descended a third staircase of thirteen feet, and passed along a corridor of thirty-six feet, and a fourth staircase of seventeen feet, and crossed a small room of twenty-four feet by thirteen. He then entered the third and principal hall, of which the first half is upheld by six columns, and the second half has an arched roof. This hall, including its two parts, is fifty-eight feet long by twenty-seven feet wide. In the second half of this hall, under the vaulted roof, marked D in our plan and section, stood the sarcophagus. Whether the king was buried in this is unknown, because it had already been violently opened and its cover broken to pieces, and no remains of the body were found there when Belzoni reached it.

Out of this hall there are six passages. On each side are two smaller rooms, in which were some wooden statues four feet high, with a circular hollow inside as if to contain a roll of papyrus. At the end is a room, in which was found the mummy of a bull, buried there probably at the same time with the king, and a countless number of small wooden figures of mummies six or eight inches long, with some few made of baked clay, with a surface of glazed blue. One of these wooden figures, bearing this king's name, is published in Egyptian

Inscriptions. Plate 71. One of blue porcelain, which may also have been found in the tomb, is in the British Museum.

The total length of the passages, from the surface of the ground to the room which held the sarcophagus, is three hundred and twenty feet, and their perpendicular depth one hundred and eighty feet. And lastly, from the floor beneath the sarcophagus descended another staircase three hundred feet in length, so far blocked up with rubbish that it has never been explored to the end.

Among the mythological sculptures on the walls of the tomb, we will mention one class as important, because less common than the others. They represent the king affectionately embracing the gods; see Fig. 2, where he throws his arms round the god Osiris. Most of the ancient Pagan nations boasted that they were beloved by their gods; the Egyptian kings styled themselves—some "Beloved by Amun," some "Beloved by Pthah," and some "Beloved by Neith;" but in this sculpture, the king, in a less usual way, declares that he loves the god in return for the blessings granted to him. His son also, the great Rameses II., who is usually styled Amunmai, or Beloved by Amun, is in

Fig. 2.

the same way sometimes styled Miamun, or Lover of Amun. This throws much credit upon the religious feelings of the Egyptians. We afterwards, in Alexandria, meet with the name Philammon, a translation of this last name; but out of Egypt, it is not till after the spread of Christianity that we meet with names showing that their bearers felt any love for their gods.

Other sculptures on the walls are nearly the same as those which we now examine at our leisure on the sarcophagus.

The sarcophagus, for the sake of which this beautiful tomb had been tunnelled into the limestone rock, and the broken pieces of its cover, Belzoni removed and brought to England. After some little time, Sir John Soane bought it of him, and then presented it to the nation, together with the other architectural and antiquarian objects in his museum.

THE SARCOPHAGUS OF OIMENEPTHAH I.

Together with the broken pieces of the lid, Belzoni brought out of the tomb a piece of alabaster, part of a square box or chest, ornamented with a female figure, standing at the corner, whose arms are stretched out backwards, so that each arm lies on one of the two sides, which join and make the corner of the box. This, however, can have formed no part of the sarcophagus.

ON THE KING'S NAMES.

Both of the names of this king are variously spelt upon the sarcophagus, and yet more variously upon his other monuments. In Plate 19 we have given five ways of spelling his first name, Nos. 77-81, and nine of spelling his second name, Nos. 82-90. The second name is that to which we attempt to give a sound, because it is that which is used by the Greek writers. On our sarcophagus it always has the sitting figure of Osiris, crowned with the mitre; having a ball upon the top, and two wings or side pieces, as in Nos. 82, 87, 88, and 89. But the earlier forms of the name have the sitting figure of Anubis, with the head of a square-eared dog, as in Nos. 84, 85, and 86. On some change of religious opinion this square-eared dog was no longer popular, and in the name, No. 90, from the Flaminian obelisk at Rome, we see how his figure was cut out, and covered up by the figure of a hawk-headed god. This change of feeling towards the square-eared dog took place in Thebes in the middle of this reign. It did not take place so soon in Ethiopia. In the temples of Abousimbel made in the next reign the square-eared dog at first received his due honour, though his name and figure were afterwards cut out by the chisel, probably before the end of that reign. The change of this character in Oimenepthah's name made little change in its sound, as the figure of Anubis was an A, and the Osiris an O. Manetho calls this king Amenophath, which agrees very well with name No. 84, spelling it Pthah, A, I, M, N, and reading it Aimenepthah. It will be observed that in so reading it we remove the word "Pthah" from the beginning to the end of the name. For this we have full authority in the other kings' names. Those of Hophra,

Nephra, Menophra, Mykera, and others, all have the syllable "Ra" first among the hieroglyphical characters within the ovals, while it ends the names as they are written by the Greek authors. But we prefer calling our king by the name No. 82, which is the later form, Oi-men-pthah or Oimenepthah. This would seem to have been the name read to Diodorus Siculus, except that his interpreter gave to the figure of Osiris the force of Os, and read it Osi-men-pthah, which Diodorus wrote Osymandyas. Eratosthenes writes this same name Cho-mae-phtha, and translates it, "The world beloved by Hephaestus." This is to be explained, first from the Egyptian use of a guttural, a doubtful breathing, between Ch and Th, which led the interpreter to pronounce our O as Cho, and which also led him to translate it as Tho, *the world*. And again it needs, as the further explanation, that we take into account their slovenly habit of not pronouncing the N at the end of a syllable. This is seen on comparing our first names, No. 79 and No. 80, one of which has an N in the syllable MEN, and the other has not. The square-eared dog was the Abyssinian

Fig. 3. The Fenek.

Fenek of Fig. 3; and by the side of it is the hieroglyphic copied from it by the Egyptian sculptor.

The name No. 86 is larger than the rest, and is Amunmai Aimenepthah. The name No. 85 is a contraction of this; and without the help of the former, the latter could hardly be explained.

In the first name, No. 79, the sitting figure is the goddess Me, or Mo, *Truth*; and the whole may, perhaps, be read Memeura. But as the Greek authors do not use this name, its force is of less importance. The change in the order of the characters in the names No. 80 and

No. 81 shows great irregularity in the way of writing; as does the separation between the letters M and N in some of the second names; while in others these letters come together. In the names No. 77 and No. 78 we have some additional characters, of which the sound is uncertain; but those in No. 77 may be translated, "Approved by the god Ra;" and those in No. 78, "son of the god Ra."

In the Appendix will be seen three lists of the names of the great kings of Egypt, ending with that of Rameses II.; the first from Eratosthenes, the second from the sculptured monuments, and the third from Manetho. By a comparison of all the names, it can be shown that our king is the one named Amenophath by Manetho, and Chomaepthah by Eratosthenes; and hence arises the support to our reading his name Oimenepthah.

ON THE AGE OF THE SARCOPHAGUS.

The dates in the earlier part of Egyptian history are very uncertain. They rest, in the first place, on a recorded Babylonian eclipse of the moon, which happened in the year B.C. 721, the first year of the reign of the Babylonian king, Mardoc Empadus, or Berodach Baladan. While this king was reigning in Babylon, Hezekiah was reigning in Judea, and Tirhakah in Egypt, as we learn from 2 Kings xix., xx.

From this period we count backwards along the reigns of the Jewish kings, till we come to Rehoboam, the son of Solomon, who was reigning at the same time with Shishank of Bubastis, king of Egypt. (See 1 Kings xiv.) Shishank was the first king of Lower Egypt who made himself master of the whole kingdom after the fall of the great Theban monarchy. This was about the year B.C. 975.

Thus far we have travelled backwards along the stream of time with tolerable certainty; but here doubt begins. Before the time of Shishank, Egypt had been governed for about twenty reigns, or 500 years, by the great Theban kings, who made the statues and built the temples for which the valley of the Nile is so remarkable. One of these was our Oimenepthah I., the father of Rameses II. Of those less important kings, who reigned before these twenty, we have not now to speak: our difficulty lies with the unimportant kings who reigned after them, because their want of importance leaves us unable to count the reigns between our Oimenepthah and Shishank of the year B.C. 975. It is probable that most of those who followed Rameses V. were not kings of Egypt, though they used the title, but were only the chief priests or magistrates of Thebes, while Shishank and his successors were reigning over the kingdom. If this be granted, then Oimenepthah I. and seven or eight successors may have filled by their reigns the two centuries before Shishank; and our king may have died and been buried in our sarcophagus not necessarily earlier than the year B.C. 1175.

We have also a second train of reasoning by which we can support the above, and which helps us to fix upon B.C. 1175 for the age of the sarcophagus. The Alexandrian astronomers and writers on the almanac, in the second century after the Christian era, tell us that the epoch of four times 365 years before the year A.D. 138, or the year B.C. 1322, was called the era of Menophra. If we now look through the list of Theban kings, we find that Thothmosis III. bore that name in his first oval, and he may perhaps be the king, from the beginning of whose reign these years were counted. Oimenepthah I. was his sixth successor, and again allowing twenty-five years to a reign, seven reigns will bring us to B.C. 1147 for the death of Oimenepthah I. In the present state of our knowledge greater certainty or greater exactness cannot be hoped for.

A third train of reasoning, leading to the same opinion, is founded on the belief that Zerah the Cushite, who invaded Judea in the year B.C. 944 (see 2 Chron. xiv.), was a king of Upper Egypt, called an Ethiopian or Cushite, to distinguish him from Shishank and his son, who were of Mitzraim or Lower Egypt. Ze-Ra, or *Son of the Sun*, is the common title of all the Egyptian kings; Rameses VII. is the only king who can in that half-century be believed to have had rule over both Upper and Lower Egypt; and Rameses VII. was the ninth in succession after Oimenepthah I. If, therefore, the one lived in the year B.C. 944, the other may have lived about B.C. 1175, as before conjectured.

THE SARCOPHAGUS OF OIMENEPTHAH I.

The Appendix, with the hieroglyphical names of the great Theban kings, will help to explain this king's place in the series of the great builders of the Egyptian monuments.

ON THE BUILDINGS AND MONUMENTS OF THIS KING.
THE TEMPLE OF ERREBEK.

Errebek, or, without the Arabic article, Re-bek, *the City of the Sun*, is the name of a village and ruined temple in the district of Gournou, the most northerly part of Thebes, on the west bank of the river. The temple was begun by this king, Oimenepthah I., and finished by his son, Rameses II. Its plan will explain the greater number of the Egyptian temples. (See Fig. 4.) It was entered through a doorway, formed of two large square-built towers. This opened into a courtyard, which was crossed through an avenue of sphinxes, nine on each side. This led to a second doorway between two other large towers, and this into a second courtyard of the same size as the last, which was crossed through a second avenue of eighteen sphinxes. This led to the grand portico of ten columns in a row, upholding a flat roof. (See Fig. 5.) Every column is in imitation of a stick or post, formed by tying together several stalks of papyrus, of which the unopened buds

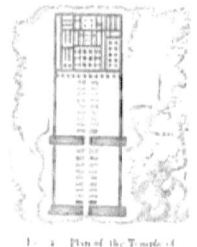

Fig. 4. Plan of the Temple of Errebek.

form the capital. The bands which tie them together are immediately below the capital. At the bottom are seen the leaves which enclose the stalk of the natural plant. Each column stands on a flat round base. The chief room in the covered part of the temple is the hall, whose roof is supported by six columns. Out of this various smaller rooms opened, in which dwelt the priests, and, at times, perhaps the king. It was dedicated to Amun-Ra, *the Sun*, the king of the gods, and to his son Chonso. The whole of the walls are covered with painted sculptures, representing the religious ceremonies, and chiefly the king making his offerings to the gods on behalf of the nation.

When this temple was built, the architectural custom had not yet been introduced of placing a low wall between each pair of columns, to

Fig. 5 Portico of Erehtak

bar the gaze of the people on the outside. This change of style in the building came into use in the next reign; and it shows an increased claim of power by the priests, who thereby made the separation between themselves and the laity more marked.

THE HALL OF COLUMNS AT KARNAK.

The old temple of Karnak was the work of many reigns. The oldest part is that built by Osirtesen I. Other kings added largely to it, and ornamented it with sculpture, statues, and obelisks. When Amunothph III. added the two solid towers which are now in the middle of it, and against which the great hall was afterwards built, he may be supposed to have completed it with these as its entrance towers. But Oimenepthah I. conceived the bold idea of doubling its size, by adding a new building in front, leaving the older to be the inner courts and halls. He began the great Hall of Columns, more than one hundred in number; and though he did not live to complete it, but left that task to his son, Rameses II., yet we may be sure that the large court which Rameses and his successors added in front of the hall was part of Oimenepthah's design. (See Fig. 6.)

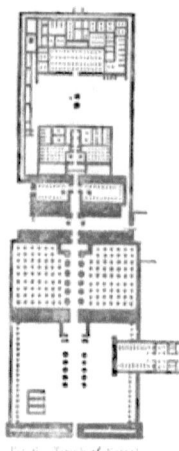

Fig. 6.—Temple of Karnak.

On each side of the walk, down the middle of the hall, is a row of five columns, of the largest size. These are 66 feet in height, and 12 feet in diameter. On each side of these, in each half of the hall, stand sixty-one smaller columns. These are 42 feet high, and 9 feet in diameter. Fig. 7 is a view along the hall between two rows of columns; those on the right are the five which form one of the middle rows; and those on the left are part of the side row next to the middle. Every column is in imitation of a plant of papyrus, of gigantic thickness; the larger columns have the capital in imitation of the flower when full blown (see Fig. 8), and the smaller columns have the capital copied from the unopened bud of the same flower (See Fig. 9.)

THE BUILDINGS IN ABYDOS.

At the city of This, called by the Greeks Abydos, this king began two important buildings, both of which he left unfinished, and they were finished by his son. One was a palace, called by Pliny (lib. v. 11) the Palace of Memnon, meaning of Miamun, or Rameses II.; and the other was a temple dedicated to the god Osiris. Abydos, or This, had been the capital of a little kingdom, and when it became subject to the kings of Thebes, it was a second capital. It was here, in the temple of Osiris, that Rameses II. set up the Historical Tablet, a list of his predecessors on the throne, which is now in the British Museum. It is from this tablet that we have copied, in our Appendix, the first names of the last seventeen kings, those of Rameses II. and his sixteen predecessors.

Fig. 2. Hall of Columns, Karnak.   Fig. 3.

THE FLAMINIAN OBELISK

This obelisk, which stands in the Piazza del Popolo in Rome, was made by Oimenepthah I., though, like the temples of Errebek and Abydos, it was finished by his son Rameses II. It is 87 feet 5 inches high. On each side are three lines of hieroglyphics. Of these the middle line was carved in honour of Oimenepthah, and the two outer lines in honour of Rameses; except on the east side, where all the three lines are in honour of Rameses. Thus we must suppose that, at the death of Oimenepthah, it was still lying on that side in the quarry; it had received the sculpture on the three sides which could be got at; but it had never been turned over to be sculptured on the fourth side. That was done in the reign of Rameses II., by whom also the two outer lines of hieroglyphics were added on the other sides.

On this obelisk the first character in the name of Oimenepthah was the sitting figure of a man, with the head of a dog with square ears, as described in page 5, thus spelling the name Aimenepthah. (See No. 83, Plate 19.) But at some later time this character was cut out, and in its place was cut, on the lowered surface, the figure of a man with a head of a hawk, and without the square ears, which were the mark of the former. (See No. 90, Plate 19.)

In what city of Egypt this obelisk was set up is unknown. The sculpture upon it has been drawn by Mr. Bonomi, and published in the Transactions of the Royal Society of Literature.

THE ANTIQUITIES IN THE BRITISH MUSEUM.

The only statue which we possess of this king in the national collection is one of wood, which was found in his tomb. It is rather larger than life, standing and stepping forwards. The right arm hangs down by the side, and once held a club. The left arm is raised, as if it once held a long walking staff, the staff so common in the hands of figures on the funereal tablets, where it marks the deceased man's rank as a landowner. In the Old Testament it is called the staff of inheritance. The hair was once tied in a tail behind. The feet are long and flat, with a low instep, as is usual in Egyptian statues. Unlike the stone statues, the back is free, and unsupported by a pillar or slab; moreover, in the stone statues we never find the arm thus free and separated from the side. Every Egyptian statue, from the earliest to the latest, from the Colossus to the smallest bronze, unless swaddled like a mummy, has, like this, the left leg foremost.

On the landing-place at the top of the stairs, which lead from the Egyptian Gallery to the rooms above, are three plaster casts from the Theban sculptures of this king. One is from the walls of the great temple at Karnak, representing Oimenepthah conquering his enemies. He is standing in his chariot. With his left hand he holds a bowstring round the neck of a chief; his right hand holds a sword, with which he is going to strike. The enemy are flying in crowds; some are dead, mostly pierced with arrows. They are probably Arabs. The king has no beard, perhaps because of his youth. He is about four times as tall as the men against whom he is fighting. His head is more deeply cut into the stone than the rest of the figure, as if the artist had altered it from the first design. In this sculpture the king's name is not spelt with the figure of Osiris, but in its earlier form, with the figure of Anubis, a sitting man with a dog's head (see Plate 19).

A second cast is from the side of the passage into the king's tomb, between the room n and the room o, in our plan, Fig. 1, page 2. It represents the judge Osiris seated on his throne, holding his two sceptres. Behind him stands the goddess of Amenti, the place of the dead. Before him is the king, who is introduced to Osiris by the hawk-headed god Horus. The flesh of Osiris is painted blue, the colour of heaven, while that of the king and of Horus is red, the colour of the Egyptian men, and that of the goddess is yellow, the colour of the Egyptian women. The king has his beard cut square, and holds the same two sceptres as the god, being himself after death and judgment acquitted, and made into a god. These figures are in low relief, not in sunk relief. In cutting a passage through the soft rock, it was as easy to make the sculptured figures in one form as in the other.

A third cast, from the same passage in the tomb, is of two priests in the same unsunk relief. They are clothed with leopard skins, and are said to be beloved by Smotef, one of the four lesser gods of the dead. This god was a suitable patron for attendants in a tomb.

Among the funereal tablets in the British Museum is one, No. 146, which speaks of this king's temple or palace. It is of limestone, 57 inches high. The sculpture is divided into three parts; at the top are two jackals, each representing the god Anubis, and between them a crowned post for the god Osiris. In the second part, the deceased man, his wife, and three sons, are presenting fire and water to the judge Osiris, seated, with Isis and Horus standing behind him. At the bottom the deceased man and his wife are seated, while eight of his sons, daughters, and relations are making the same offerings to him, as he was in the line above making to the gods. He was a scribe belonging to the army, and attached to the palace of Oimenepthah I.

It would seem that no king of Egypt has received credit for any of the great works which he began, unless he lived to put his own name upon them; and Oimenepthah may have begun others besides these mentioned. The great court-yard at Karnak, and its towers at the entrance, were certainly his design, though not bearing his name, because his Hall of Columns would have been incomplete without them. The numerous colossal statues, and the obelisks of his son Rameses II., seem too many to be the work of one reign; some of them were most likely begun by the father. Had the temples of Abydos, of Errebek, the Hall of Columns at Karnak, and the Flaminian obelisk, been only a little less forward at the time of his death, they would all have been thought the work of Rameses II.

THE ALABASTER SARCOPHAGUS IN SIR JOHN SOANE'S MUSEUM.

This beautiful stone coffin was formed of two parts, the chest and the lid, each hollowed out of a single block. The stone is white and translucent, allowing the light to shine through it. It was dug from the quarries at Alabastron, a town on the east side of the Nile, which has given its name to the stone. Blocks of any size may be there obtained.

The lid, or cover, has been broken into numerous pieces, of which there are seventeen in the Museum. It was itself a hollowed block, which, when placed upon the chest, added 15 inches to its height.

The chest is slightly shaped to the body, or rather to the inner cases, which were so shaped. It is narrower at the head and foot than in the middle, with a slight increase of width above the shoulders, marking the great size of the hanging folds of the shawl which covered the king's head. The bottom of the chest and the top of the lid are also narrower than the middle. There is a slight swell on each side for the calf; and a small swell equally well marked for the ankle. The outside measures of the chest are—

Length, 9 feet 4 inches.
Greatest breadth, 3 feet 8 inches.
Breadth at foot, 23¼ inches.
Breadth at head, 22 inches.
Height without the cover, 32 inches at the shoulders, and 27 at the feet.

The thickness of the stone is from two and a half to four inches. Of this thickness the inner half at the upper edge of the chest is sunk about three-quarters of an inch, and the lid has the outer half sunk to match; thus making the chest and its lid fit more closely. This is shown in Plate 17. At the foot of the chest, on this sunk ledge, has been engraved

DIS^D BY G. BELZONI.

Both the chest and the remains of the lid are covered inside and out with small figures, and hieroglyphical writing engraved upon the flat polished surface; and at the bottom, within the chest, is a figure of the goddess Neith, *the heavens*, larger than life, engraved in outline, there lying to embrace the embalmed mummy, or rather the wooden mummy case, which was to be placed within the sarcophagus. All the engraved lines and figures were at one time filled up with blue paint, made of some preparation of copper. This has in many cases fallen out; and what remains has mostly been made black by the London smoke, which has at the same time discoloured the white alabaster.

Whether the lid was ever fastened on does not now certainly appear. The fastening, however, if any, must in any case have been very slight. But it would seem as if some little violence had been used to separate the lid from the chest, because the edge of the chest is broken in several places, particularly near the left shoulder and left ankle and right foot. It would seem as if an iron tool had been applied to the left shoulder to wrench off the lid, and that the weight of the lid, when lifted from that spot by the lever, had broken the edge of the chest on the opposite side, near the right elbow, and also at the right foot.

It might be supposed that the chest and the lid had once formed a single block, and that they had been sawed asunder after the outside had been cut into shape. But from the veins in the stone this seems not to have been the case. Indeed, it would be equally easy for the sculptor to have begun by placing the two squared and solid blocks one upon the other, and thus have shaped the outside of both at the same time. When so shaped outwardly, the two blocks must of course have been separated, to be hollowed out and to have the small figures cut upon them.

There is a slight crack in the chest of about 14 inches in length, near the right elbow. It runs downward from the upper edge, beginning in the hieroglyphics of line 33, Plate 4. Whether this crack was made by the original sculptor, or by those who broke the lid off afterwards, is uncertain.

A small round cavity near the back of the head of the goddess Neith, at the bottom of the chest, see Plate 16, betrays the manner in which the mason worked. It is about the sixteenth of an inch deep, and seven-eighths of an inch in diameter. It was made by a drill, but made unfortunately rather deeper than it should have been. The mason, having cut the outside of the block to its proper size and shape, would seem to have drilled a number of holes downwards, into the body of the stone, to a given depth, and thus he may have lessened the risk of splitting the alabaster with his chisel. Had he attempted to hollow out the sarcophagus with no other tool than chisel and mallet, the danger of splitting the stone would have been very great. The foot or end of the chest is perfectly flat, having been cut by a saw; and at the lower part of the end there are the traces of the fracture, the rough portions left when the other piece of stone broke away, called by the masons "the saw-break."

On the outside of the lid, on the lappet of the shawl which covered the king's head, are three smaller drill holes, each a quarter of an inch in diameter. They touch one another, and thus make one larger hole, No. 16 Q, in Plate 19. They were probably made to receive some metal ornament; but as no other portion of the flat top of the lid remains, it is useless to conjecture their purpose more exactly.

The stone is so far brittle that it must have required no little skill for the makers to place the heavy lid upon the chest without injury to the edges. To guard against such an accident they would seem to have shielded the edges of both chest and lid with a thin plate of copper. The reason for so thinking will be understood from the section of the edges in Plate 17.

There it will be seen that four thin grooves run round the whole sarcophagus, two on the chest, and two on the lid, each at the distance of about an inch from the edge. In these grooves there still remain small pieces of the metal. Had the grooves been only on the outside of the sarcophagus, we might have supposed that the metal reached from the groove on the lid to that on the chest, and thus formed a slight fastening. But in this way we cannot explain the use of the two grooves on the inside. The metal can only have been hammered into them before the chest was closed by the lid. Hence no other supposition offers itself for the use of these grooves, but that they received the strips of metal which were to guard the edges from injury, as represented in one of the sections on that Plate.

When the delicate edges were thus guarded, the lid was probably lifted on to the chest, and placed in position, by means of cords, which passed, not round it, but through holes, of which we have three remaining. Of these one is seen on the right side at G, the second is in the fracture between G and the head of Thoth, in Plate 18; and the third on the left side, at B C, Plate 19. The portions of the lid which received the three corresponding holes are missing. Each hole is seven-eighths of an inch in diameter, being made by the same drill as that already spoken of as making the slight cavity at the bottom of the chest.

The sculpture on the outside of the chest is divided into several portions.

First there is a single line of hieroglyphics running all round at the upper edge, making two sentences, each beginning on the right side of the head, and ending at the left side of the foot. Below this line of writing is a band, one inch wide, which also runs round the whole chest. It is covered with engraved dots, once filled with the same blue copper paint. It was perhaps meant to represent the firmament of heaven; though in Plates 4 and 5 dots of the same size are clearly used to mean the earth; and in this respect they may be compared with the Hebrew word Shehak, which means at the same time small dust and the skies.

The sculpture beneath this line of dots is divided into five sets of pictures, of three in a set, by five tall doors, each turning upon two pivots in the place of hinges, and each guarded by a serpent which looks over the top.

The first door is on the right side at the head.
The second door is on the same side at the hip.
The third door is on the same side at the foot.
The fourth door is on the left side at the foot.
The fifth door is on the left side at the elbow.

Beneath these pictures is a second dotted band of the firmament, one inch wide, speckled with blue dots like that above, showing that the pictures between them represent events which are to take place not on earth, but after death. The doors are those of Amenti or Hell, and they are spoken of in the book of Job (xxxviii. 17), where the Almighty asks, "Have the gates of death been opened unto thee? or hast thou seen the doors of the shadow of death?"

On the inside of the chest the pictures are again in the same way surrounded by the dotted blue bands of the firmament, and divided into sets by doors. One band of blue dots runs all round the upper edge, and a second below divides the pictures on the four sides from the picture at the bottom. These two bands are united at the left side of the head, by a similar band running from top to bottom, in the middle of which is a round ball to represent the sun, which is travelling along this its path. Beginning at the right side of the head, instead of one door there is a pair, each turning on a pair of pivots, and shutting, so as together to close a doorway doubly wide.

The second door is on the right side at the hip.
The third door is at the end against the right foot.
The fourth door is on the left side at the hip.
The fifth door is on the same side at the cheek.

These five doors, or six, as the first two were a pair, have each a tall serpent looking over the top as a guard, but they do not, like those on the outside, put out the cloven tongue.

On the bottom is a large figure of the goddess Neith, engraved in outline, and surrounded by lines of hieroglyphical writing; some over her head, even between the large letters of her name, others by her side and between her arms and her body, and others under her feet.

To judge from the broken pieces of the lid which remain, the sculpture upon it was of the same character as that on the chest. On the outside a single line of hieroglyphics ran round the bottom edge, divided into two sentences, each beginning at the right side of the head, and ending probably at the left foot. On the sides above this are several pictures with small figures, and hieroglyphical writing over them. At the top there once lay a figure of the king larger than life, of which no parts now remain except the right flap of the shawl which covered his head, and the ends of several feathers near, which show that two winged divinities lay upon his body, of which we have many examples on the mummy cases in the British Museum. It would seem as if the aim of the person who broke the lid into pieces was to carry away this figure of the king, after breaking off the side pieces which we now possess, as adding unnecessarily to the weight.

On the sides of the inside of the lid are other sculptured pictures; but whether any one large figure was on the inside of the roof is doubtful. If there was such a figure, it had on its breast a scarabæus, or perhaps a vulture, with outstretched wings, of which we have a part remaining, on the piece marked r, in Plate 18, which on the outside carries the end of the king's head-shawl.

We sometimes see in a sarcophagus the figure of Isis, the goddess of earth, lying at the bottom of the chest, and the figure of Neith, the goddess of the heavens, lying opposite to her on the inside of the lid. But as here Neith lies at the bottom, and as the top would have been an unsuitable place for Isis, it is not probable that any second large figure was there sculptured.

DESCRIPTION OF THE PLATES. (*Plate 1.*)

The four views of the sarcophagus in the upper line show the whole of the outside. The subjects of the sculptures begin with the line (u v) on the right-hand side of the head, and thence continue round the chest, and end on the head.

The four views of the sarcophagus in the second line are sections showing the sculpture on the inside. These begin at the place where the others began, at the right-hand side of the head, and end at the same place.

The subjects on the outside and on the inside of the chest are each fifteen in number, contained in five pictures of three subjects each. These pictures are divided by tall doors guarded by serpents. In each picture, in the centre compartment of the three, we find one view of the boat of the god Ra.

The three views in the bottom line of this Plate show the goddess Neith lying at the bottom of the chest, and also two restorations of the lid; one of the outside and one of the inside. The views of the restored lid show the pieces which are now in the Museum. To every one of these its place can be certainly assigned by the help of the sculptured figures. The small piece marked 2 in Plate 19, containing the lappet of the king's head-dress, explains to us that the head was ornamented like the usual statues of the kings. The pieces of the wings in Plates 18 and 19 tell us that the king had a winged sun on his head, and two winged animals, probably vultures, on the breast on the outside, and one winged animal, probably a ram, on his breast on the inside. The jackals' tails also on the fragments call for the restoration of the whole animals on the inside of the lid. This restoration is shown in Mr. Bonomi's drawing.

THE SCULPTURES ON THE OUTSIDE. (Plates 2-8.)

First, we have a single line of hieroglyphics running round the upper edge, divided into two sentences, each beginning at the right-hand side of the head, and ending at the left-hand side of the foot. In these the deceased king declares, on the right-hand side, in Plate 2, that he is Amset, the son of Osiris; that he is Anubis, whose mother is Isis; in Plate 3, that he is Sotef, the servant of Osiris.

On the left-hand side, in Plate 8, he declares that he is the son of the goddess Neith, and of the god Mo, or *Truth*; and that he is Hepi; in Plate 7, that he is Anubis, and that he is Snouf.

Amset, Sotef, Hepi, and Snouf are the four lesser gods of the dead, whose names and heads are upon the four Canobic jars, in which the softer parts of the body are preserved (see Fig. 10). These gods

Fig. 10.— Four gods of the dead.

befriend the deceased on his trial before the judge; they sometimes present offerings to the judge, as mediators on his behalf; and they are sometimes sacrificed for him, and he places them on the altar as his atoning sacrifice. Anubis, with the head of a dog, is the god who has charge of the mummies. Into these gods the king now declares himself changed.

Beneath this upper line of writing there is a band of blue dots, representing the sky, and below the sculptures there is a second band of dotted sky, telling us that the whole of the pictures between them are of events which take place in another world.

The sculpture is divided into five portions. Each begins with a door which turns upon two pivots for hinges, and is guarded by a tall serpent, styled the appointed door-keeper and guard. Beyond the door, in four of the five pictures, is the garden of paradise, surrounded by two rows of cypress trees, trees which do not grow in Egypt. The garden is guarded at each corner by a sacred asp of the cobra capella kind, with swollen chest, who spits fire around the garden wall. This serpent is the Uræus, or basilisk, and is the serpent of goodness. Within the garden lie the mummies of good men, who are declared to be gods and goddesses.

A single line of hieroglyphics divides this garden from three long pictures, over each of which are about fifty short lines of hieroglyphics. In these vertical lines the characters are placed in the usual order, so that the reader begins with the face of the animals; but the lines themselves are placed in the less usual order, so that in moving from line to line the reader follows the animals instead of meeting them.

FIRST PICTURE (Plates 2-3.)

Within the garden, or after passing it, the picture is divided into three parts or rows. At the top we meet with the corn growing in the inundated land. It is bearded wheat, and with it are twelve granaries, or heaps of corn, each crowned with the head of a god: these are the gods of the grain. Beyond are twelve mansions, or monastic cells, with two doors each, within which the good men are dwelling. These are guarded by a fiery serpent of the same kind as that which guards the door to each picture, or division of the chambers of death. Cultivation of corn, in a well-watered field, was thought to be one of the employments of the blessed after death.

In the middle of the picture is the boat of Kneph-Ra dragged in sacred procession. The god has a ram's head, because he is Kneph, *the spirit*; and he has the sun on his head, because he is also Ra, *the sun*. He is two persons, making only one god. He stands in the boat under a canopy, probably a gnat-gauze, and over that is the Eternal Serpent, one of the forms under which the heavens are represented. Before him is a guard, and behind him the steersman with his two rudders.

The sacred boat is pulled by a rope held by four men, which is fastened to a pole carried by eight bearers, which again is fastened to a second rope pulled by four more men. The pole has a bull's head at each end, and on it stand small statues of two bulls and seven sitting men, who are called the Egyptian gods. Beyond these men, who are all pulling along the sacred barge, stand four more men bandaged as mummies.

At the bottom of the picture we see the giant serpent, named Apoph, with its numerous folds. This is the serpent of wickedness, the enemy of the human race. On one side of it stand nine men, called the slayers of the serpent Apoph; and on the other side is a man or god leaning on his staff, the mark of his rank, like an overseer with his nine workmen. Beyond are nine other men, or rather gods, each holding in one hand the character for life, and in the other an Anubis staff, or rod, with an animal's head. These are styled other conquerors, having taken part in the battle against the giant serpent; and before them is a second overseer, or master, leaning on his staff of rank, or staff of inheritance, as it is named in Jeremiah x. 16 and li. 19.

We are reminded of this wicked serpent in the book of Job, where we read of the Almighty in chap. xxvi. 13:—

"By His Spirit he garnished the heavens;
His hand wounded the crooked (or cowardly) serpent."

SECOND PICTURE. (Plates 3-4.)

Here we have the tall door, as before, guarded by its serpent, the garden with its rows of fir trees, and asps at the corners, and the nine mummies lying within the garden.

In the upper part of the picture is a row of twenty-four men.

In the middle of the picture is the boat of Kneph-Ra, drawn by four men, and met by two men, then by the gods Kneph and Horus, and then by nine others, followed by the overseer with his staff.

At the bottom of the picture is a row of twenty wicked men, each with his arms tied behind him, awaiting his punishment. Beyond lie four good men enjoying their ease, and beyond them stands the overseer leaning on his staff. On some of the painted papyri, these good men are each lying by the side of a water tank, which is a most desirable luxury in a warm climate. Here their tanks are not drawn; their happiness is shown only by their lying at rest, and the characters at their feet tell us that they are good.

THIRD PICTURE. (Plates 4 and 5.)

This is less than any of the other pictures, and is limited to the foot of the sarcophagus. Here the tall door, guarded by the serpent, is not, as in the other cases, followed by the two rows of cypress trees. The picture is not divided into three parts. It contains a view or section of the world in the form of a flat valley between two hills. But this valley is cut in half, and one half is turned with its face downwards over the other half. On one half stands a pole with the head of Kneph, the ram, and on the other a pole with the head of Anubis, the dog, each between a pair of kneeling men. This last pole, like the hill on the same side of the valley, is turned downwards, and the kneeling men beside it have their heads downwards. By the side of each pole is written, " The image of the corn-land." Over the upper half of the valley are twelve men, named the gods of the corn-lands; and under the lower half are twelve other men, named the gods of the corn-lands of Amenti, or the place of the dead.

In the middle, between the upper and the lower land, is the boat of the god Ra, in which the god is represented by a ring or ball for the sun, on which is its name, a scarabæus. The serpent, instead of forming a canopy over the god, is here made to encircle it, with the tail in its mouth. As in the other pictures of this boat, there is a guard at one end, and a steersman at the other.

The dots sprinkled over the tops of the two hills may be compared with " the highest part of the dust of the world " in Proverbs viii. 26.

THE FOURTH PICTURE. (Plate 5, 6, and 7.)

First we have a tall door, turning upon two pivots. A long serpent, the guardian of this door, looks over the top.

On passing this door, we enter a paradise or garden, with a row of fir trees on the top, which makes it probable that it is situated in a country far to the north of Egypt, as on the banks of the Nile such trees are unknown. Here sits the judge, Osiris, wearing the double crown of Upper and Lower Egypt, holding in his right hand Life, and in his left the crozier. The legs of his throne are formed like lions' legs, a form afterwards imitated by the Greeks for their chairs. Before him stands the great pair of scales resting upon a man's shoulders. In this the doings of all mortals are to be weighed. In one scale it is usual to see the heart of a deceased man, and in the other scale the figure of Truth. But here we have the soul in the form of a bird instead of the heart, and the artist has put nothing in the other scale. Above is the dog-headed god Anubis, whose duty is to bring the dead into the presence of the Judge. Below are nine men, the representatives of the human race, mounting the steps towards the judgment seat. In front of the Judge is a boat, in which an ape, one of the keepers of the fiery pit, is carrying away a wicked man, who has been changed into the form of a pig. Other wicked men are on their knees beneath the Judge's throne, working with axes, as if condemned to the mines. A pig is the unclean animal into which the souls of the wicked were sometimes said to migrate; and on the painted papyri we see that the souls of good men are sometimes sent into the body of a ram, the animal sacred to the god Kneph, *the spirit*.

Leaving the garden of the Judge, we enter the garden of the blessed, as in former pictures. This is fenced with two rows of the same fir trees. At the corner of each is a serpent of goodness, the *cobra capella*, known from the serpent of evil by its enlarged chest. Within this garden lie the mummies of good men, who are declared to be now changed into gods and goddesses. They are twelve in number.

We then come upon the three rows of figures, as in the former picture, and thus remark that the garden of the Judge, with the interesting scene of mankind coming to judgment, is placed between the tall door and the garden of the blessed, which two in most of the other pictures touch one another.

In the upper part of the picture we have the great serpent carried along like a coil of rope by twelve men who have conquered it, and followed by twelve other men in the act of bowing to it, and met by four gods, each carrying an Anubis staff.

In the middle of the picture we have a god before whom are standing twelve men; behind these are nine others, the conquerors of the great serpent, which they are carrying in their arms; and these are followed by the boat of Kneph-Ra, drawn along by four men.

At the bottom of this picture are, first, eight men, then twelve carrying the serpent, and then sixteen others with the hawk-headed Horus leaning on his staff, as the overseer. These sixteen are in four groups, of four each; they are often met with on the monuments, and often variously coloured and dressed, showing that they are meant for four races of men.

FIFTH PICTURE (Plates 7-8)

After the door and its serpent, and the mummies lying in the garden of paradise, we have, in the upper part of the picture, a river with two bridges, described as the Bridges of Life. Twelve dog-headed gods are named the keepers of the Bridge of Life. Before them are ten serpents with swollen chests, the Serpents of Life; and behind them are twelve figures of men, declared to be gods.

In the middle of the picture is the great serpent of evil, with its numerous folds, standing in the river, with six women standing on each bank. Beyond is a temple with nine cells, in each of which lies a mummy. The building is a flat roof upheld by ten columns. Beyond, again, is the boat of Kneph-Ra, drawn by four men.

At the bottom of the picture are four doors, the entrances of tombs.

beside which stand the door-keepers, one with an Anubis staff, and four others bowing forward. Then are twelve gods; then the god Osiris standing as conqueror upon the serpent of evil, which may be considered as the earliest form of our well-known group of St. George and the Dragon, or of holiness trampling down sin. In front of Osiris stands a serpent of goodness, followed by twelve gods, the last of whom is Horus leaning upon his staff as the overseer.

THE SCULPTURE ON THE INSIDE. (Plates 9-15.)

Here we have not got the single line of hieroglyphics, which runs round the upper edge. In other respects the inside is much the same as the outside. It contains five pictures divided by doors, but in this case there are six doors to the five pictures, as the first and the last pictures are separated by a pair of doors.

SIXTH PICTURE. (Plates 9 and 10.)

After passing through the door, guarded by its serpent, we come to the garden with its two rows of trees, within which, in place of the mummies in the former pictures, we have two poles; on the top of each is a human head, and above one is the sun, and above the other a scarabaeus. After this, in the upper part of the picture, we have a god with a crocodile's head, followed by eight goddesses, each sitting on an Uraeus, then by twelve gods, each carrying an Anubis staff. Of these, four have hawks' heads, four rams' heads, four human heads. Then follow four more, each holding up a star in the right hand; and then four, each holding up a sun in the right hand.

In the middle of the picture we have a god followed by a goddess of Lower Egypt and a goddess of Upper Egypt, being so distinguished by their crowns. Then are four apes, each holding up a large human hand. Then the great serpent, named Apoph, *the giant*, tied to the ground by several chains. In front of it stand nine gods with swords as though to attack it; four have dogs' heads, and five have human heads. These are followed by four men drawing the boat of Kneph-Ra.

At the bottom of the picture we have a god with a cat's head holding an Anubis staff, followed by four men in the attitude of bowing, four women standing uncrowned, four with the crown of Lower Egypt, four with that of Upper Egypt; four men uncrowned, four with the crown of Lower Egypt, again four uncrowned, and lastly, four with the crown of Upper Egypt. These men represent the four well-known ranks in the Egyptian priesthood, and hence the women may represent three ranks of priestesses.

SEVENTH PICTURE. Plates 40 and 41.

Here, within the garden, we have two Anubis staffs, one with the crown of Upper Egypt over it, and the other with that of Lower Egypt.

Beyond this, in the upper part of this picture, we have first a serpent with a chain round its neck. The chain is held by four men, and a fifth man seems to lie upon the chain; but he is perhaps only so placed because the artist, from not understanding perspective, wished in this way to represent him as on the other side of the serpent. This chained serpent is attacked by eight men with swords. Four of these men have human heads, and four have each a fourfold serpent's head. Five other serpents are all tied to one chain, which is held at one end by a human hand rising out of the ground, and by twelve men, or gods; and at the other end by five other men, or rather gods, who, by a false aim at perspective, are made to lie upon the chain. These are the god Seb and the four mediating gods of the dead, Amset, Hepi, Sotef, and Snouf. Behind these stands Osiris, Rhot-amenti, *king of hell*, whence came the Greek name Rhadamanthus.

In the middle part of the picture, we have the boat of Kneph-Ra drawn along by four men. Before these walks a man holding up on high a star in his right hand. Before him four figures are seated on the ground; one with a hawk's head, one with a cat's head, and two with human heads. Of these two, one has long hair, and the other is baldheaded; they both have beards, though all the four figures sit upon their heels, with both knees on the ground in the attitude more common with the women. Then we have three men, each holding up a star with one hand, and with the other holding the rope of a boat, in which is a human head, and an Uraeus serpent. Next is a serpent rising from the ground with its two wings out-stretched, as in the act of flying. This may be the Seraph, or winged serpent of the Hebrew writers. Next is a man holding in his hand what seems to be a flame of fire, which he pours upon the top of a post, having a ram's head and horns. Next is an Uraeus standing upright on its tail, having three heads, two human, and one that of a serpent. This three-headed serpent is worshipped by four women, who hold up both their hands toward it in prayer. Lastly is a god, a union of Horus and Anubis, with two heads, one a hawk's, and the other a square-eared dog's, and with two pairs of hands. He stands upon a platform made with two bows, and the tails of six Uraeus serpents.

In the bottom part of the picture we have a large eye, placed upon a bird-perch, before which stands a god with an Anubis staff. Behind this is an ape on a second perch. Before him stand four gods, two with human heads, and a star on each head, one with a stag's head, and one with a crocodile's head. Each holds an Anubis staff, and the character for life. Behind them stand twelve women holding to one cord, each has a star on her head. These are the twelve hours. Behind these are twelve men, each holding an oar, or pole enlarged at the end.

EIGHTH PICTURE. (*Plates 12 and 13.*)

Here, within the garden, we have a row of twelve asps or serpents of goodness. Then in the upper part is a hawk-headed sphinx wearing the crown of Upper Egypt. From the tail end of its body rises a man's head with the same crown. On its back stands the two-headed god of the last picture (Plate 10), at once Horus and Anubis. On each side of this are five men holding a rope; the four pull against the one. The one has a bald head; the four have serpents' heads, and are crowned, but the crown rests not on the serpent, but on the man's shoulders.

Between the one man and the four on each side of the sphinx is a sloping pole, with a crowned head. And we may remark, in respect to the two races of men who inhabited Egypt, that the head with the Theban crown has a short beard, and the head with the Memphite crown has a long beard. The human head at the tail of the sphinx, with a Theban crown, also has a short beard. Beyond this a man between eight serpents, each with a pair of human legs; four walk to the right and four to the left, while their eight tails meet together in his hands. Beyond this is another man in the same way holding the tails of eight serpents with human legs, four walking in each direction. These eight serpents have human heads. Two other crowned serpents, each turning its back towards the eight serpents and the man, have their tails meeting at his feet. A group of two men, each holding an open sling or rope held by both hands, stand apart by themselves.

In the middle part of the picture we have as usual the boat of Kneph-Ra, pulled along by a rope held by four men. In front of these walk six men holding slings. In front of them are four apes holding slings. In front of them are four women holding slings. In front of them are three men holding spears, and each holding at the same time the curling folds of a cloth which covers a man who is crouching upon his hands and knees before them. This man hidden under the cloth, and the figures behind him armed with spears and slings, are advancing to attack two great monsters; one is the giant serpent Apoph, and the other is a crocodile whose tail ends in a serpent's head, and who turns this tail against his assailants.

On the lower part of the picture we have a crowned hawk, seated upon the folding tails of four serpents. Of these, one on each side of the hawk is a serpent of evil walking on human legs, and the other, the Uraeus, the serpent of goodness. Under this group passes a long rope held on one side by eight men and on the other by sixteen men; of these last, four have rams' heads representing the god Kneph, four have hawks' heads for the god Horus, four have birds' heads for the god Thoth, and four have human heads, and are declared to be souls in Amenti.

NINTH PICTURE. (Plates 13, 14 and 15.)

Within the garden are nine mummies.

In the upper part of the picture we have a god standing, who is worshipped by nine human souls, each in the form of a bird, with the head and hands of a man. On our title-page we have a man and his soul under the same form, receiving knowledge from the goddess of the sacred tree. These nine souls are followed by twelve men standing.

In the middle line we have a river or piece of water, in which are sixteen figures of men in four groups of four each, in various attitudes. These are spiritual beings or ghosts. They are named Mout, *the dead*, Nouf, *the spirits*, Achu, *the magicians*, and Erepo, *the water-spirits*. This last is the same as the Hebrew word Rephaim, and reminds us of the passage in Job xxvi. 5, "Spiritual beings are born under the waters, and are the inhabitants thereof." Beyond the piece of water is the boat of Ra drawn along by four men holding the rope.

In the bottom line we have the great fiery serpent with seven gods, his keepers, standing upon his folds, while twelve wicked men, with their arms tied together at their elbows, are brought up by a keeper to be destroyed by the blast of fire which this great serpent breathes out upon them from his mouth. This dreadful animal seems to be meant by Job in chapter xxvi. 13, when he says, "God by his spirit garnished the heavens, his hand formed the crooked serpent."

TENTH PICTURE. (Plate 15.)

This is one of the smallest pictures, being of the same size as that at the foot of the sarcophagus on the outside. It contains only one subject. Here the dotted band of the sky which runs round on the top of the pictures is united to that at the bottom of the pictures by a vertical band of the same width; and that it is the sky or pathway of the sun is shown by the figure of the sun which is here met with upon it.

In this picture we have a representation of the ocean, in which float both the circular world and the boat of Ra, the sun. But the attempt to show the sun at the same time in its two positions, as held up by the sky in the daytime, and by the ocean at night, is a little confusing.

In the boat, the sun, with the scarabaeus as its name, is attended by Isis, Nepthis, Seb, and seven other gods. The boat is upheld by the hands of the god of the ocean, of whom we only see the bust from the breast upwards. The air, or empty space above the boat in which the figures stand, is joined to the band of sky which runs round the whole of the inside of the sarcophagus.

Thus far we have described the picture as it stands upright. We now turn it the other way, and we see the circular figure of the earth surrounded by Osiris. It is a plane floating upon the waters, as described in Proverbs viii. 27:

> "When God prepared the heavens, I, Wisdom, was there;
> When he drew a circle upon the face of the deep."

and again in Job xxvi. 10:—

> "He drew a circle upon the face of the waters
> As a boundary between light and darkness."

Upon the head of this figure of Osiris stands the goddess Neith, the supporter of the sun, which she upholds with her outstretched hand. The artist makes one figure of the sun answer two purposes, as it is thus held up on one side by the goddess Neith, while on the other side it is in its boat supported by the figure of the ocean.

After learning from this picture that the figure of a man, holding over his head the sun, is meant for the god of the ocean, we may carry our knowledge to explain one of the pictures on the funereal papyri. These papyri frequently contain a group of four pictures, placed one over the other in a column. In the first the deceased person is in the boat of the god Ra. In the second is the sun, with rays of light streaming from it. It is between two worshippers; sometimes they are both goddesses of Amenti, but at other times they are the deceased person and his wife. In the third we have this figure of a man, or more often the bust of a man, holding the sun upon his head by help of his two hands. The sun sends out no rays. On each side of him is a soul, in the form of a bird, with human head and hands, and two, or perhaps four, monkeys. These all hold up their arms as in the act of prayer. One of the birds has a beard, showing that it is the soul of a man; the other has not, being the soul of his wife. In the fourth picture we see the deceased man and his wife, both seated, with a table of offerings set out before them, and a priest presenting fire and water to them as if they were gods. These four pictures, with some slight variations, may be seen on many of the funereal papyri.

The third of these pictures receives its explanation from this sarcophagus (see Fig. 11). Here we have the sun supported by the ocean:

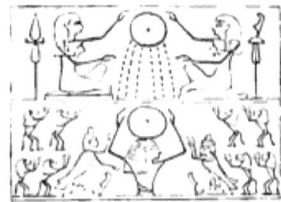

Fig. 11.

it is therefore after sunset, and beneath the earth. It sheds no rays, and it may be contrasted with the sun in the second picture, which sheds numerous rays. This, which we may suppose is in the heavens overhead, is worshipped by the man and his wife in bodily form, but the former sun which is upheld by the ocean, we must suppose to be in some unknown dark place beneath the earth, where it gives no light, and where it is worshipped by the souls of the two deceased persons.

Again, these pictures on the papyri explain to us that the circular earth on the sarcophagus (Plate 15), is not an island standing up out of the water, but is like a raft floating upon its surface, as the sun, when in the ocean, is supposed to be beneath the surface of the earth. And this is further supported by passages in the Hebrew writings, such as Psalm cxxxvi. 6, saying that God stretched out the earth over the waters; and the ten commandments, which speak of the fish in the waters beneath the earth; and yet more exactly does Proverbs viii. 27, already quoted, describe this circular plate of the earth floating on the ocean.

F

THE BOTTOM OF THE CHEST.

(Plates 16 and 17.)

At the bottom of the chest lies a large figure of the goddess Neith. She is standing with arms straight, and hands open to receive the body of the king. The face and lower parts of the body below the waist are in profile, but with a front chest, front shoulders, and a front eye. She has two right feet, they both show only the great toe. The eyebrows and eyelashes are painted. As the drawing is little more than an outline, one breast only is shown; the artist has not known how to represent the second. From the Egyptian figures of this class, it would seem as if the Greeks had borrowed the notion of a race of Amazons, or women with one breast. The goddess has long hair falling partly in front and partly behind, and tied back from her eyes by a riband or diadem. Her dress is a tight robe reaching from the ankles to the breast, and held up by two shoulder-straps, each fastened with a buckle on the shoulder. This robe is formed of feathers, and over it are closely folded a pair of wings, like those of the cherubs over the ark in the Jewish temple. In this way is shown the heavenly character of the lady. She wears round her neck a collar formed of nine broad bands, the lowest of which is of beads. She has broad anklets round the legs, bracelets round the wrists, and armlets round the upper part of the arms.

In order to explain the proportions which the Egyptian artist gave to the human figure, her height has been, by Mr. Bonomi, divided into nineteen parts, by lines on the margin of the Plate, which show that the artist worked according to the usual Egyptian canon, as shown on the accompanying woodcut (Fig. 12). Counting downward from the head, the divisions are as follow:—

No. 1. At the bottom of the forehead.
 „ 2. At the bottom of the nose.
 „ 3. At the top of the shoulder.
 „ 7. At the narrowest part of the waist.

THE SARCOPHAGUS OF OIMENEPTHAH I.

No. 9. At the widest part of the body.
„ 10. At the wrist as the arms hang down.
„ 12. At the tips of the outstretched fingers.
„ 13. At the top of the knee.
„ 17. At the bottom of the dress.
„ 18. At the top of the instep.

Above the head of the goddess is her name written by means of three large characters N T for Neith, and the figure of the heavens

Fig. 12.

covered with stars to help out and explain the very insufficient spelling, which without that sign might have many other meanings. The N is a vase partly full of wine, and it seems to prove the use of glass at that time, as it is transparent. The T is a half-circle, the figure of a hill, and takes its force from the word TEI, *a hill*.

The writing with which the goddess is surrounded is wholly in praise of the king, and very much made up of the same thoughts and sentences repeated again and again. Thus, line 1 begins with "Honours to the deified King, Lord of the world * * * lately deceased, son of the Sun, Oimenepthah deceased," line 21 contains the same words, ending at the right shoulder. Lines 15 and 16* both begin with the same words, and, with variations, the same is found in lines 20, 29, and 30. Other sentences begin as in line 6, with "Honours to Seb;" in line 25, "Honours to Neith the great goddess." Others as in line 26, "I am Neith;" in lines 32 and 29, "I am the son of Athor." The king's soul is mentioned under the figure of a bird with a human head, in lines 17*, 25, and 28, and in 19, as "the illustrious soul of the changed deified king deceased." Much of this is clearly written to fill up the space; it is used as ornament, as we see the larger hieroglyphics used on the architectural parts of a temple. In lines 4 and 28, the king has the title of Sethon, written by means of a twig, a small semicircle, and a wavy line. This priestly title, which may be translated *king*, is used by Herodotus as the name of the general who fought under Tirhakah against Sennacherib. It is also the word Sethos, which Manetho gives as a title of Rameses, as we shall see in the Appendix, when comparing Manetho's kings with the monuments.

In Plate 17 we have sections of the edges of the lid and chest, showing how they are made to fit; and showing also the four grooves, or notches, which run all round the sarcophagus, and the copper casing which we have conjectured was once there as a guard to save the edges from being broken.

BROKEN PIECES OF THE RIGHT SIDE OF THE LID (*Plate 18*).

The pieces on this side all join together and form part of one continuous picture for the outside, and of a second continuous picture for the inside. Those at the top of the plate show us the outside. Round the bottom runs one continuous line of writing, which, like the line on the top of the outside of the chest, is in praise of the king. The writing is to be read in two directions, beginning at the dotted line u-v, which marks the corner of the sarcophagus, and the division between the head and side. The dotted line w-x, divides the head from the shoulder. Above the single line of hieroglyphics is a band of blue dots, probably representing the firmament, and above that is a picture divided into three parts, but broken at each end.

In the upper part we have six men, each with the ostrich feather of truth on his head; and then four men, with what may be a flower on the head. They all hold up their hands as if to support these objects.

In the middle part we have six posts, each having a dog's head, and to each of which are tied two criminals. Between each pair of posts stands a mummy-shaped man, except between one pair, where there are two large human eyes. Beyond is a man leaning on a staff, the usual attitude of an overseer who has the charge of these criminals, and behind him are two men holding a rope, probably part of the company pulling along the boat of the god Ra.

In the bottom part of the picture is a man carrying a ploughshare, and behind him are six large ears of corn standing out of the ground, the bearded wheat, or *Triticum compositum*, of Egypt. Towards each of these, a man is stooping as if going to gather the harvest. These are evidently good men, happily employed in agriculture after death, as those in the former row were wicked men, awaiting the punishment that their crimes deserve.

The fragment marked k is the only piece that we possess from the roof of the lid. Upon it are the sculptures of the inside surface. The portion of wing probably belonged to a vulture, perhaps having the head of a ram, which had its place over the king's breast. The broken lines of hieroglyphics are in honour of the king.

Those on the bottom of the plate show us the sculptures on the inside of the fragments we have been describing. The few lines of hieroglyphics which remain are probably all in praise of the king, and not like those on the outside of the same fragments, which relate to the events in the next world common to all mankind. Here the principal figure is the god Thoth, having the head of an ibis, and a cow's tail hanging down behind from his waist, a common ornament with Egyptian kings. In his hand he holds a rope, which hangs down from the hieroglyphical character for the heavens, and at the bottom of the rope is fastened a lamp. In this way the stars are frequently represented as lamps hanging from the sky.

Above the head of the god Thoth is the tail of a large jackal, whose body was on the roof of the lid. The position of this animal, and of the great wings of which we here have parts only, will be seen in Plate 4, where M. Bonomi has attempted a restoration of these sculptures. In this plate we see two of the large round holes, by the help of which we suppose the lid was lowered on to its place, and also four small holes marked L M N O, for which we are unable to conjecture any purpose.

BROKEN PIECES OF THE LEFT SIDE OF THE LID. (*Plate 19.*)

The pieces on this side do not form one continuous picture. Like those on the other side, we have the bottom line of hieroglyphics in praise of the king. Above it a dotted band representing the firmament, and above that the three parts of a picture or pictures. And here we are so fortunate as to have one of the doors guarded by a tall serpent, and the two rows of trees the boundaries of the garden, which tell us that the sculpture on the sides of the lid on the outside, was divided by these doors into a certain number of pictures, in the same way as we have seen on both the outside and the inside of the chest.

In the upper part of the pictures here, we have a row of men, each holding part of a rope, or, possibly, it may be of a serpent.

In the middle part we have a row of figures, of which two are standing mummies, and seven are gods, each holding an Anubis staff; behind these is the boat of the god Kneph-Ra.

In the lower part, we have a row of six men lying at full length upon couches, with their backs upwards, and holding up their heads like so many sphinxes. The couches have lions' legs, but have not, as is usual with the couches for mummies, the lion's head and tail.

The fragment Q is from the roof of the lid. The sculpture upon it is that of the outside. The horizontal bars are the pattern upon the shawl which the king wore upon his head. This portion is the flap or end which hung upon the right shoulder; but this will be better understood in Mr. Bonomi's restoration of the figure in Plate 1. Near to the Figure 16, are three small drill holes. For what purpose they were made is unknown. They have broken one into the other.

On the lower part of the plate, we have the sculptures upon the inside of the same fragments. The god Thoth, the jackal's tail, and the wing behind the god correspond to those in Plate 18. The broken lines of hieroglyphics all relate to the king. The line w-x marks the division between the head and shoulder of the sarcophagus. The line y-z marks the elbow.

On the fragment P, we see another of the large round holes by which we suppose the lid was lowered on to its place.

In this plate, fragments M and N are wrongly placed; they ought to be changed in position, as in Plate 1; each ought to stand in the other's place.

APPENDIX.

In the accompanying tabular view of the series of Egyptian kings, in pages 44 and 45, the row of hieroglyphical names, the names from Eratosthenes, and those of each dynasty of Manetho, form each an independent authority. They are here placed side by side in columns to show that, in respect of the Kings of Thebes, Manetho, Eratosthenes, and the tablet of Abydos, are all speaking of the same kings; and to prove that these authorities embrace, within the limited period of twenty-two reigns, that important portion of Egyptian history which reaches from the builders of the great pyramids to Rameses II. The names, it is true, are often unlike, nor is the order of names in each quite the same. But the disagreement in a few cases is far outweighed by the satisfactory agreement in the larger number of cases. In order to show that these several lists are here placed side by side correctly, and that they fill no more space in time than that above assigned to them, we must consider a few of the names more carefully.

1st. As to the kings of Manetho's eighteenth dynasty, we will compare the three authorities in the following manner:—

ERATOSTHENES.	THE MONUMENTS.	MANETHO.
	Chebra = Ames	1. Amosis.
		2. Chebros.
21. Echescosocara.	Sheg-beghara = Amunothph I.	3. Amenophthes.
		4. Amersis.
22. Queen Nitocris, who governed for her husband.	Mesphophra Thothmes I.	5. Misaphris.
	Mesphoph Thothmes II.	6. Misphragmuthosis.
	Mesmeso Thothmes III.	7. Tuthmosis.
23. Myrtæus Ammonodotus.	Amunothph II. Grandfather to the Maker of the Vocal Statue.	8. Amenophis of the Vocal Statue.

The agreement here is close enough to prove that neither list should be moved higher or lower, and that Manetho has made a mistake in giving the vocal statue to Amunothph II. Chebra = Ames may have been made by Manetho into two persons. Ames Athori, the wife of King Amunothph I., may have succeeded him as regent and have been counted by Manetho as a sovereign under the name of Amersis.

Eratosthenes has not names enough in his list. With a slight variation he calls

Ammunothph I. by his first name Shoshegkara, giving to the sword in his first oval the force of Shog-sheg, which is one of its Coptic names. He rightly says that Queen Nitocris will represent her husband Thothmosis II., but we also know that she governed during the first years of his successor Thothmosis III., and therefore we need not be surprised that that king also is omitted from the list, and we must consider it as an error of Eratosthenes that he has omitted the name of Thothmosis I.

The agreement of the names which follow is not so satisfactory, but is all that we could wish in the case of Semphrucrates or Amenoph, of Ramesses I. and of Oimenepthah I., the king of our sarcophagus, and of Rameses II., the first king of the nineteenth dynasty. This last was the greatest of the Egyptian kings. He is called Tyrannus by Eratosthenes, and Sethos, *the king*, by Manetho.

The names in Manetho, which are not in the tablet, may be all accounted for as being those of women. On the death of Thothmosis IV., Egypt was for a time governed by his widow Moutnes, who may be Manetho's No. 10, Acherres; and her daughter Ammo-Rathos may be his No. 11, Rathos. So also we may without violence suppose that his No. 13, Acherres, is another queen, who may have had some right to be called a sovereign. The name of Acherres may be derived from that of the goddess Athor, with the guttural ch changed into th. This would be a natural title for a queen.

2nd. As to Manetho's eleventh and twelfth dynasties, we remark that Labaris, after whom the labyrinth was named, was probably a king of Heracleopolis, and ought to be removed out of this list. There then remain five names out of seven with a very satisfactory agreement, quite close enough to prove that if we take the tablet of Abydos as an authority, Manetho's twelfth dynasty was immediately succeeded by his eighteenth, and that the intermediate dynasties were reigning, if at all, contemporaneously in other cities of Egypt.

Eratosthenes, although he by no means agrees throughout with the other authorities, yet confirms this view. His Chnubus Gneurus is clearly Noubkora or Amunmai-Thori II.; and his Moscheres is Meskora=Osirtesen III. He thus agrees with the tablet of Abydos in the close succession of all these kings, and in forbidding the introduction of any space of time between Manetho's twelfth and eighteenth dynasties.

3rd. As to the place given to Manetho's kings of Memphis and their reigning in that city contemporaneously with the twelfth and earlier half of the eighteenth dynasty in Thebes, it depends on our showing that Nitocris, the last of the Memphites, is the same person as the Nitocris of Eratosthenes, and as the wife of Thothmosis II. In support of this we remark:—

Firstly, that Minerva the Victorious is simply a translation of the Coptic Neith-chori, which we recognise as the name of the wife of Thothmosis II. By her numerous buildings we see that she well deserved the title given to her by Eratosthenes of governing the kingdom for her husband. Indeed she did the same for his successor, Thothmosis III.

Secondly, that the authority of Eratosthenes quite justifies our placing the builder of the third pyramid, as Manetho describes her to be, at this modern date, because he places Saophis I. and II., the builders of the great pyramids, at a time yet more modern than our view of Manetho places them.

Thirdly, that Nitocris, the wife of Thothmosis II., was not simply a queen-consort, is shown by the monuments, where she declares herself a sovereign in her own right by appearing very often, though not always, in man's clothes, as a king. But as her husband was king of Upper Egypt we must look elsewhere for her kingdom; and we see that Manetho explains this by saying that a queen of that name was the last sovereign of Memphis. Her marriage seems to have united the two kingdoms into one.

We further see that this arrangement places Manetho's Phiops, who lived one hundred years, at the same point of the series as Eratosthenes' Apappus, who was said to have lived the same length of time. Eratosthenes asserts, what may have been true, that four of Manetho's Memphite sovereigns for a time bore sway over Thebes; namely, Suphis I., Suphis II., Phiops and Nitocris.

We have now to consider the subject of the name found in the third pyramid. This is Mikora, or Menkora. Herodotus says that this pyramid was built by Mykerinus; but then he adds that some said it was built by a woman. This latter opinion agrees with the statement of Manetho. But further, the same hieroglyphical name was found in the fourth, a smaller pyramid. This would seem to agree with our opinion that two sovereigns at the same time had equal claim to a regal tomb. And lastly, if we compare this hieroglyphical name of Mikora, or Menkora, we shall see that it agrees sufficiently well with the first name both of Queen Nitocris and that of Thothmosis III., her second colleague on the throne, to remove all apparent contradiction. Her first name is Mikera, and his first name, which at Thebes was Menkophra, or Menkora, may easily have been written at Memphis Menkara, by a change naturally arising from the use of the guttural.

If it should be thought necessary to justify the harsh change from th to ch, which we have supposed to arise from the use of the guttural, it may be done by showing how often it occurs. Thus Osiri-tesen is in Manetho Geson goses; Neit-thori is in Eratosthenes Nitocris; Chomaepthah is translated as if it were Thomaepthah; Menhora on the Theban monuments becomes Menkora in the third and fourth pyramids; and Manetho's name for the queens, Acherres, is of course borrowed from Athor, the name of the goddess. So the crocodile which, in the east of the Delta, gave its name to the Lake Temsi, was called by the priest who talked to Herodotus Champsi. Cush and Ethiopia are both derived from the Coptic Etosh or Ethosh. By these and other instances of words written with h and th at Thebes and in the east of the Delta, being written with ch at Memphis, and by the Greeks, it seems probable that the guttural so common with the Hebrews was also in use in Egypt.

Having said thus much in support of our own views, it may be as well to mention those of other Egyptian students. Those who are in favour of a longer chronology, place all Manetho's dynasties in one continuous series; and refuse to throw aside, as we have done, six of his dynasties as filling no space of time, because they were reigning at the same time as those of Thebes and Memphis. They thus place the builders of the two great pyramids about forty reigns earlier than we do. They reject the testimony of Eratosthenes altogether, and that of the tablet, so far as it shows that there is no interval between the twelfth dynasty and the eighteenth.

Again, those who give to our king, the owner of the sarcophagus, the name of Sethos, or Seti-Menepthah, do so because they attempt to reconcile Manetho and the tablet rather differently. They disregard all the points of agreement pointed out in page 10, and, preferring the one agreement which we have felt obliged to reject as Manetho's mistake, they place the owner of vocal statue in each list opposite to that in the other. This brings down the names of Rameses or Sethos, the first of the nineteenth dynasty, to a second king of the name of Oimenepthah. And thus, without any authority whatever, they give to the sitting figure in our king's second oval, No. 84 in Plate 19, the force of Set, and call the kings Seti-Menepthah I. and II. But in page 36 we have shown that this word Sethos is one of the priestly titles given to other Egyptians, but given emphatically to the great Rameses for the same reason that Eratosthenes calls him Tyrannus.

The reader has here the whole of the materials before him to judge between these two views of Egyptian history, between what may be called the long and the short chronologies.

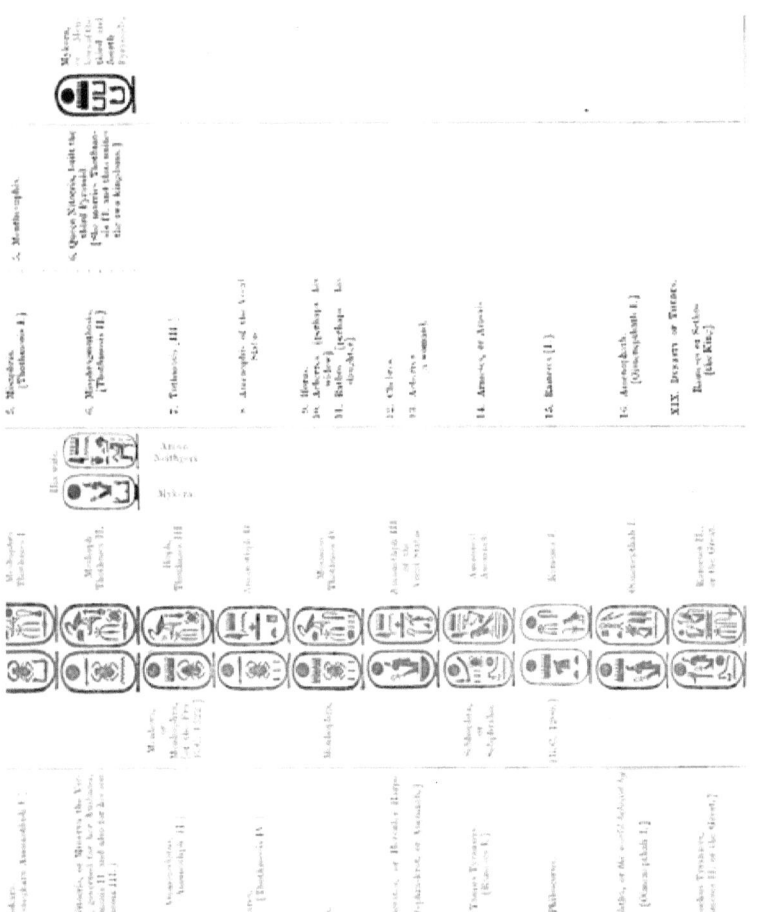

WORKS BY THE SAME AUTHORS.

THE TRIPLE MUMMY CASE OF AROERI-AO, AN EGYPTIAN PRIEST; in Dr. Lee's Museum, Hartwell.

THE CHRONOLOGY AND GEOGRAPHY OF ANCIENT EGYPT.

WORKS BY JOSEPH BONOMI.

THE PROPORTIONS OF THE HUMAN FIGURE ACCORDING TO THE ANCIENT GREEK CANON OF VITRUVIUS. Second Edition.

NINEVEH AND ITS PALACES. Third Edition.

WORKS BY SAMUEL SHARPE.

THE NEW TESTAMENT TRANSLATED FROM GRIESBACH'S TEXT. Fifth Edition.

CRITICAL NOTES ON THE AUTHORIZED ENGLISH VERSION OF THE NEW TESTAMENT.

HISTORIC NOTES ON THE BOOKS OF THE OLD AND NEW TESTAMENTS. Second Edition.

THE HISTORY OF EGYPT FROM THE EARLIEST TIMES TILL THE CONQUEST BY THE ARABS in A.D. 640. Fourth Edition.

ALEXANDRIAN CHRONOLOGY.

EGYPTIAN INSCRIPTIONS FROM THE BRITISH MUSEUM AND OTHER SOURCES. 216 Plates in Folio.

EGYPTIAN HIEROGLYPHICS: being an Attempt to Explain their Nature, Origin, and Meaning. With a Vocabulary.

EGYPTIAN ANTIQUITIES IN THE BRITISH MUSEUM DESCRIBED.

EGYPTIAN MYTHOLOGY AND EGYPTIAN CHRISTIANITY: with their Influence on the Opinions of Modern Christendom.

PLATE 1

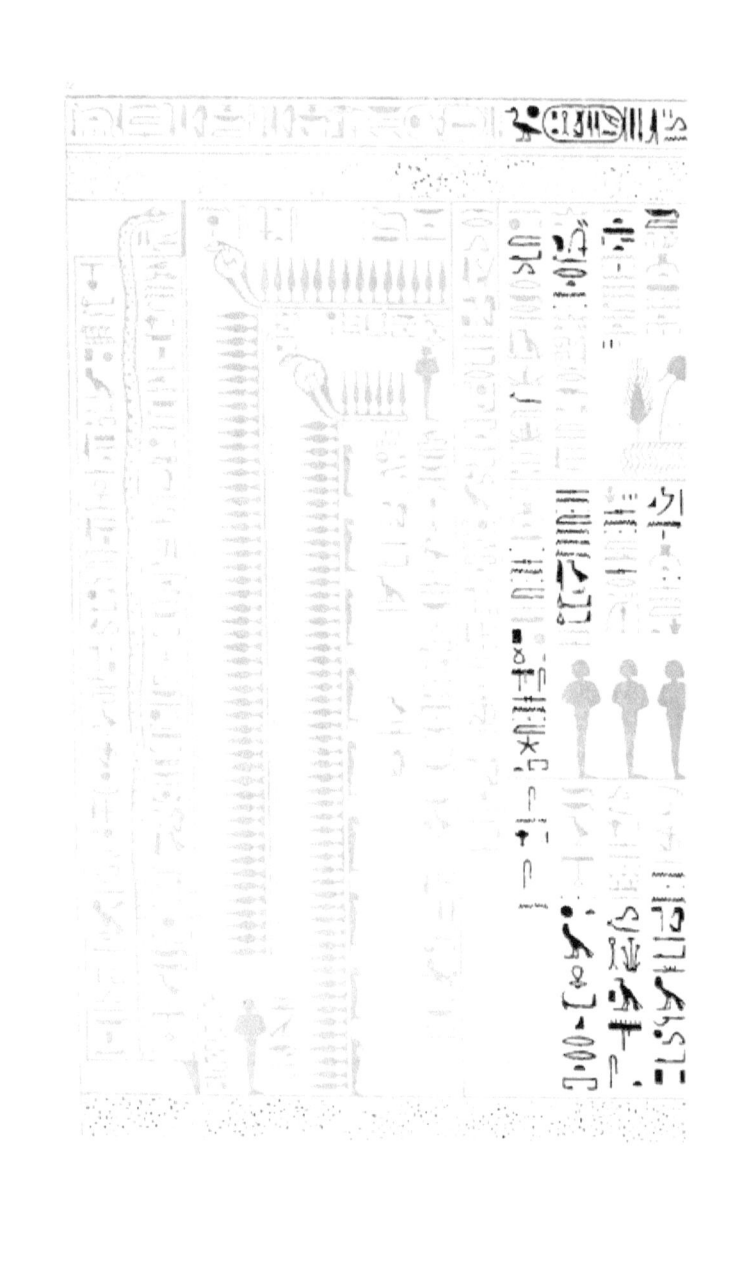

PLATE 2

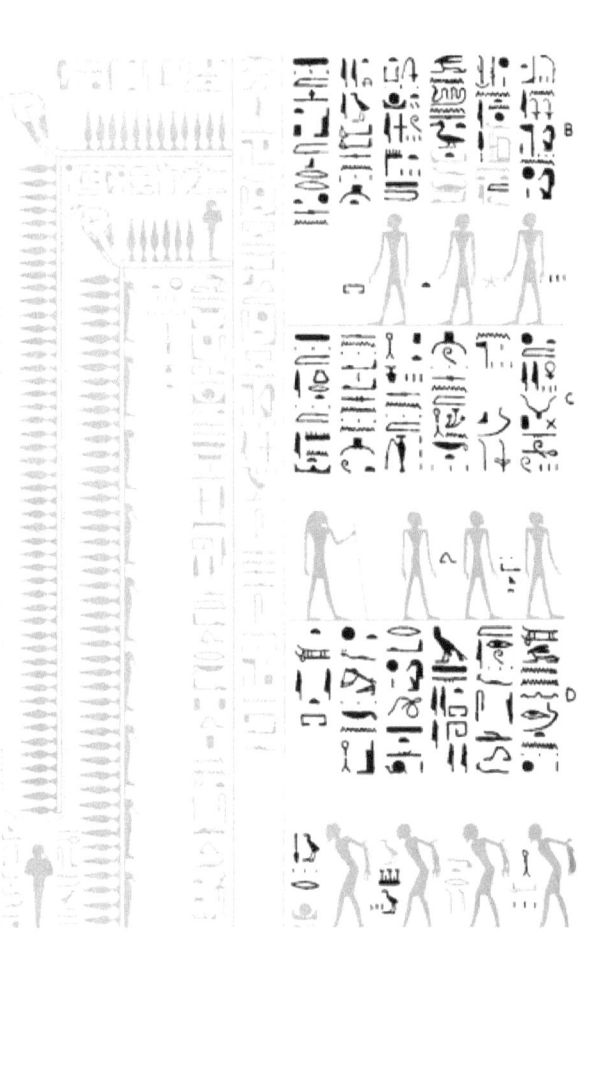

B

C

D

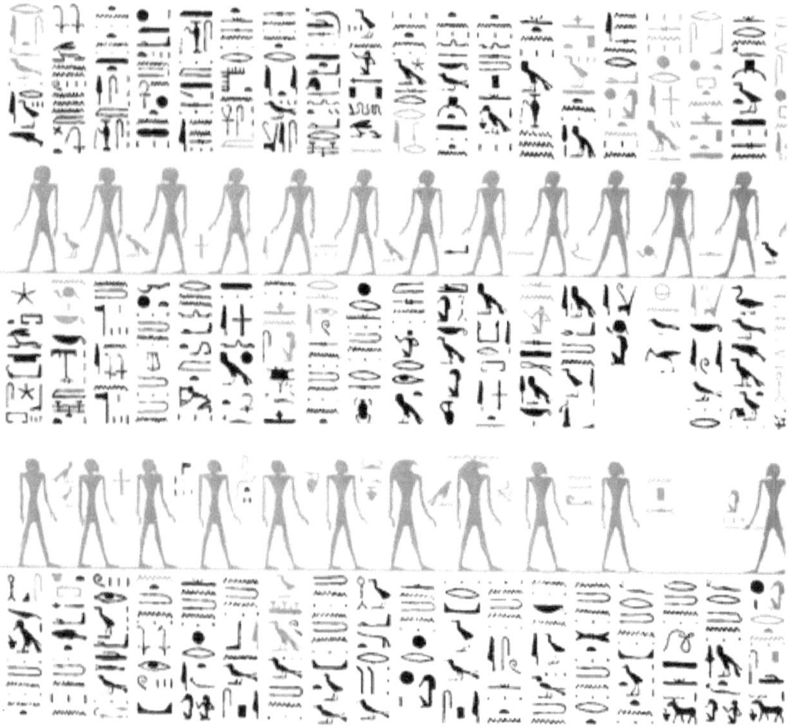

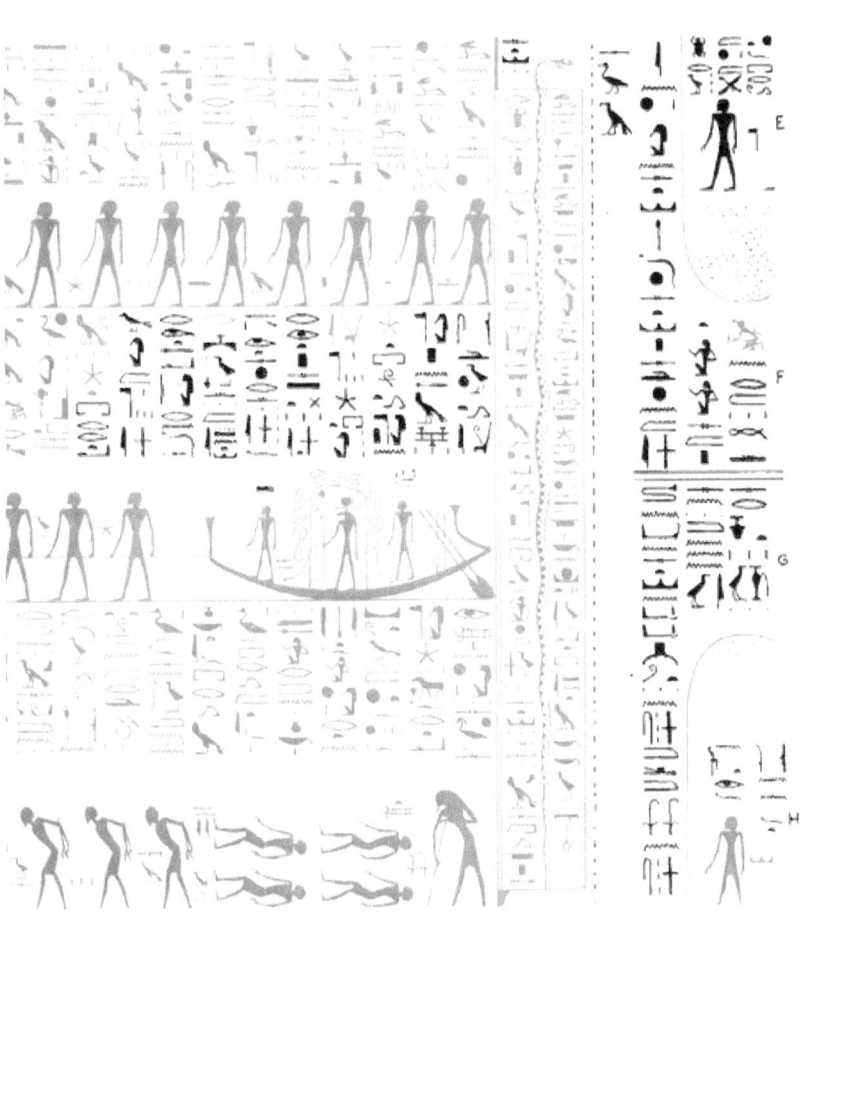

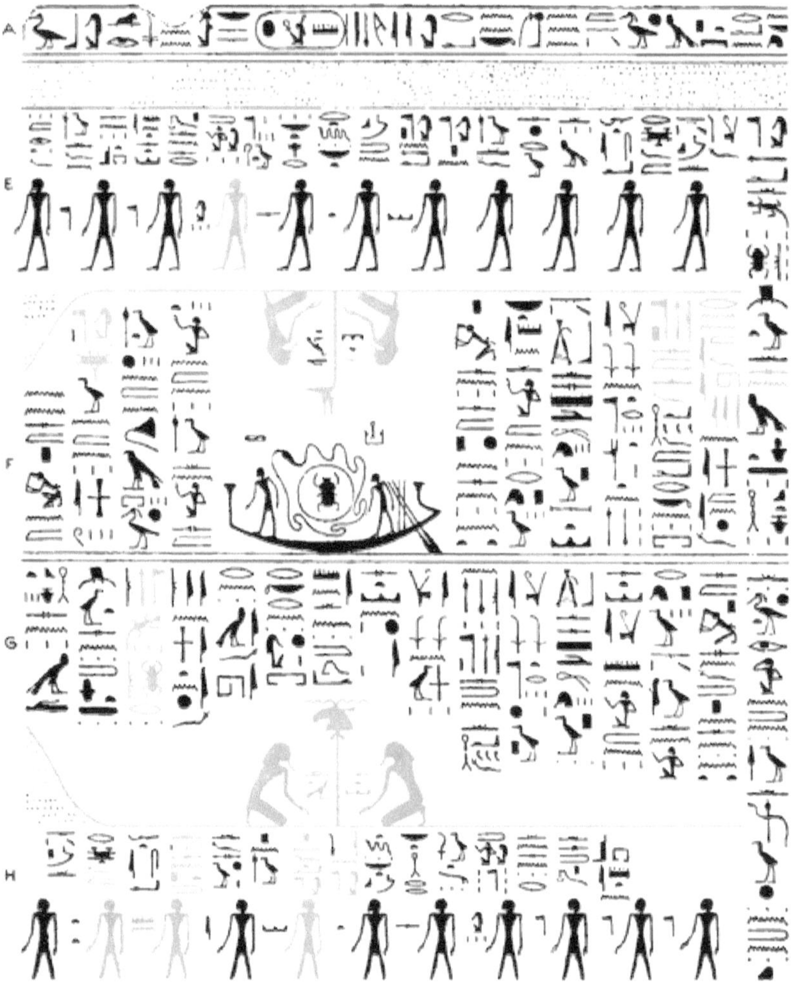
A
E
F
G
H

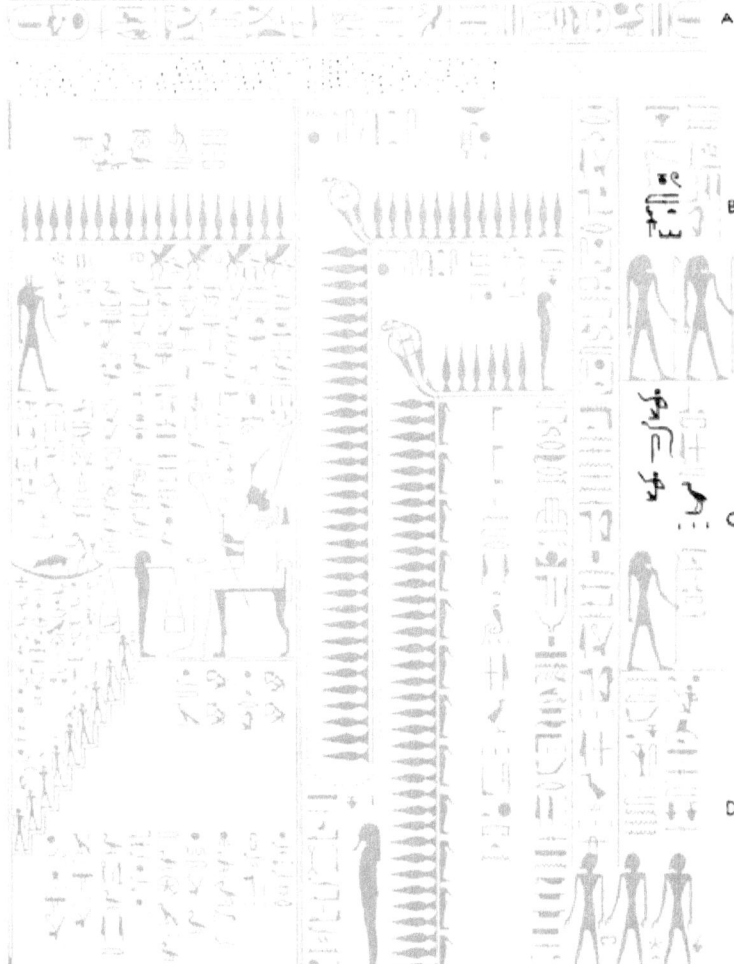

PLATE 5

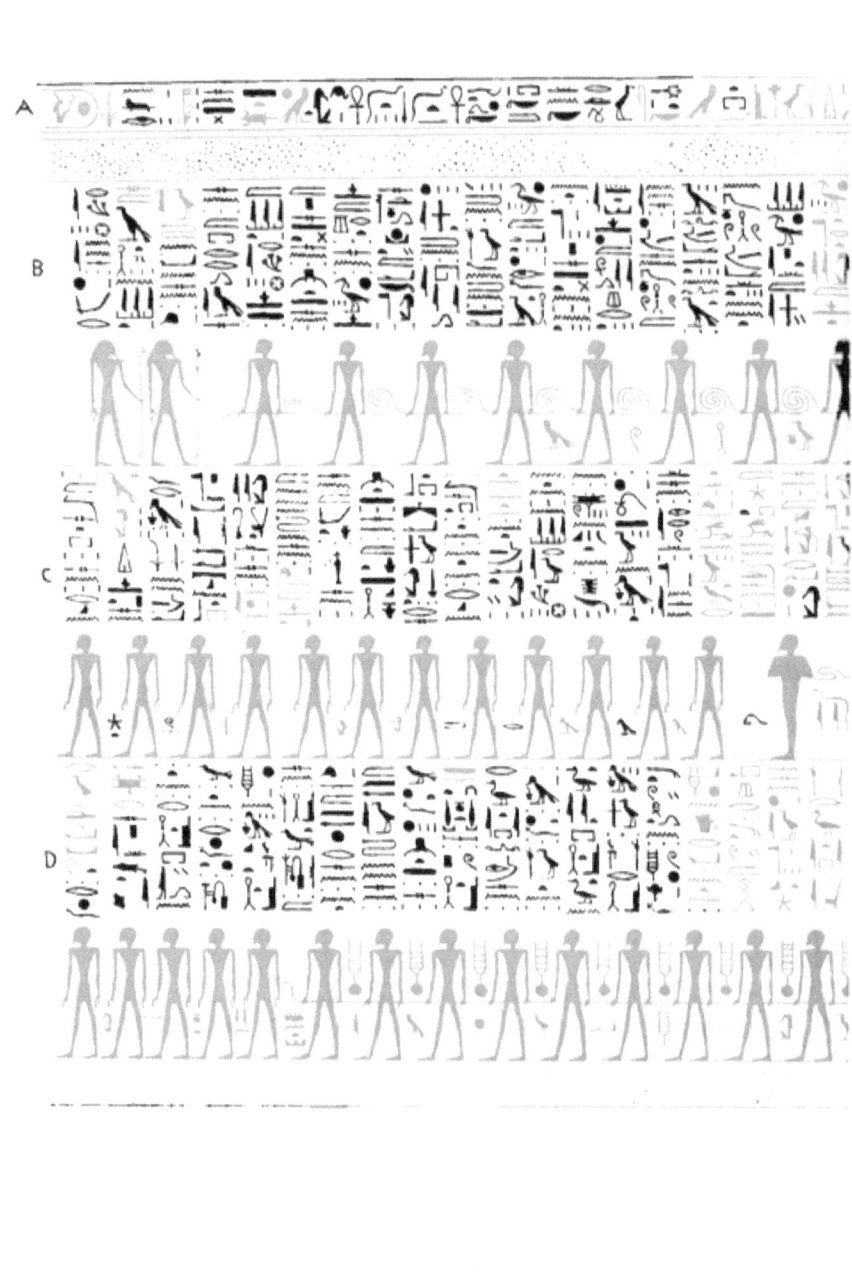

PLATE 6

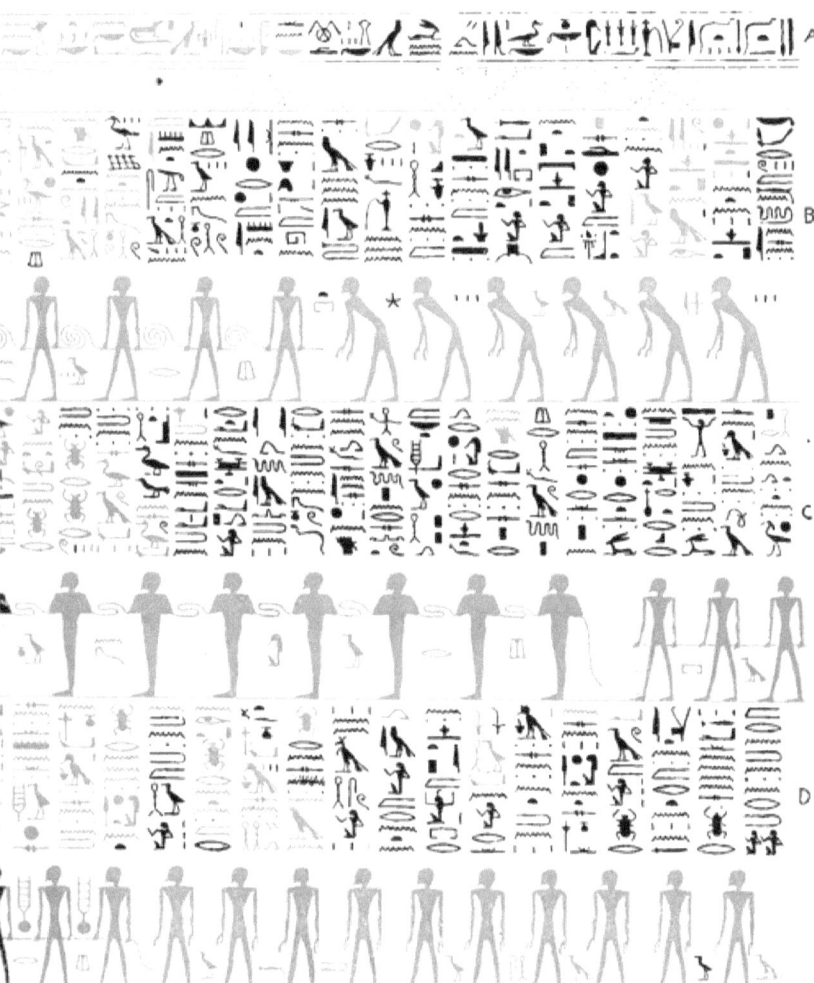

y'

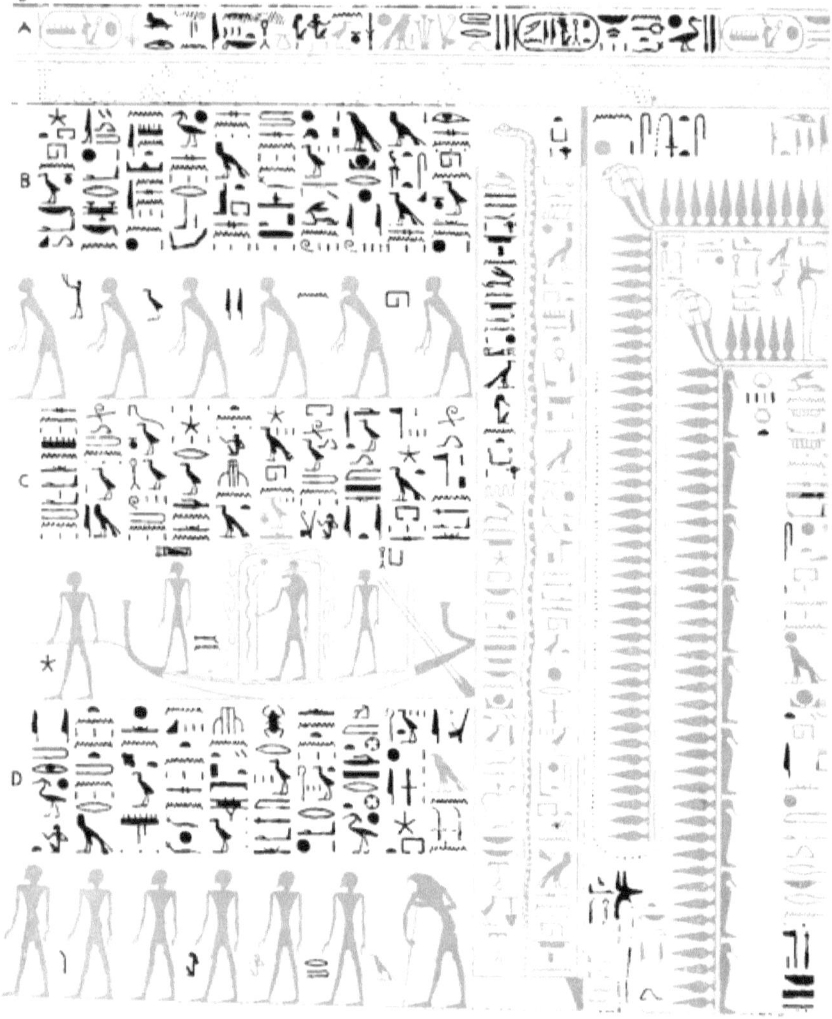

PLATE 7

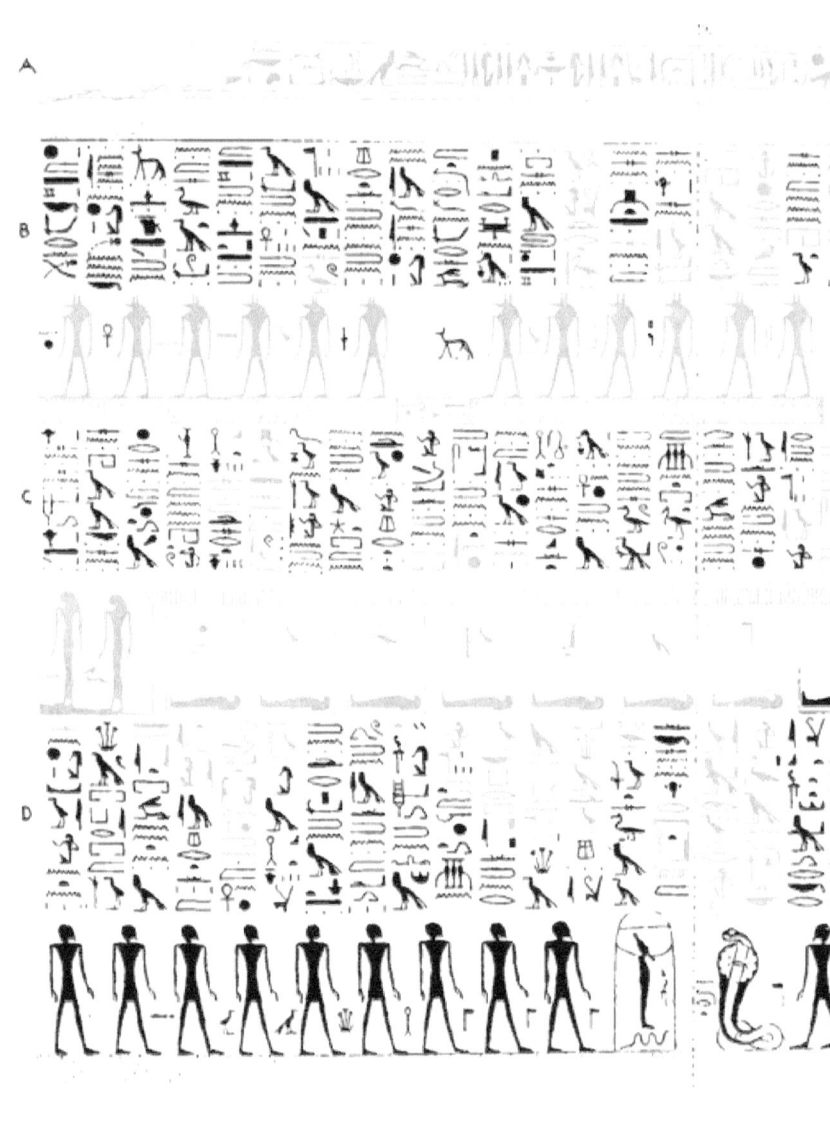

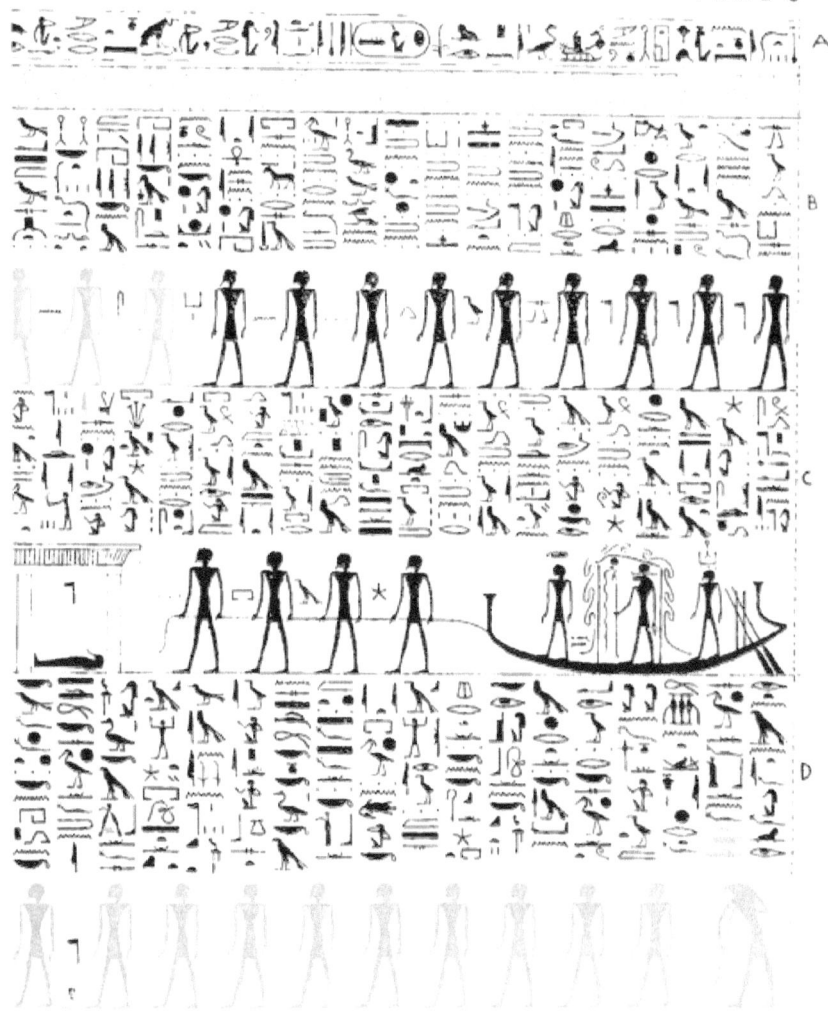

PLATE 8

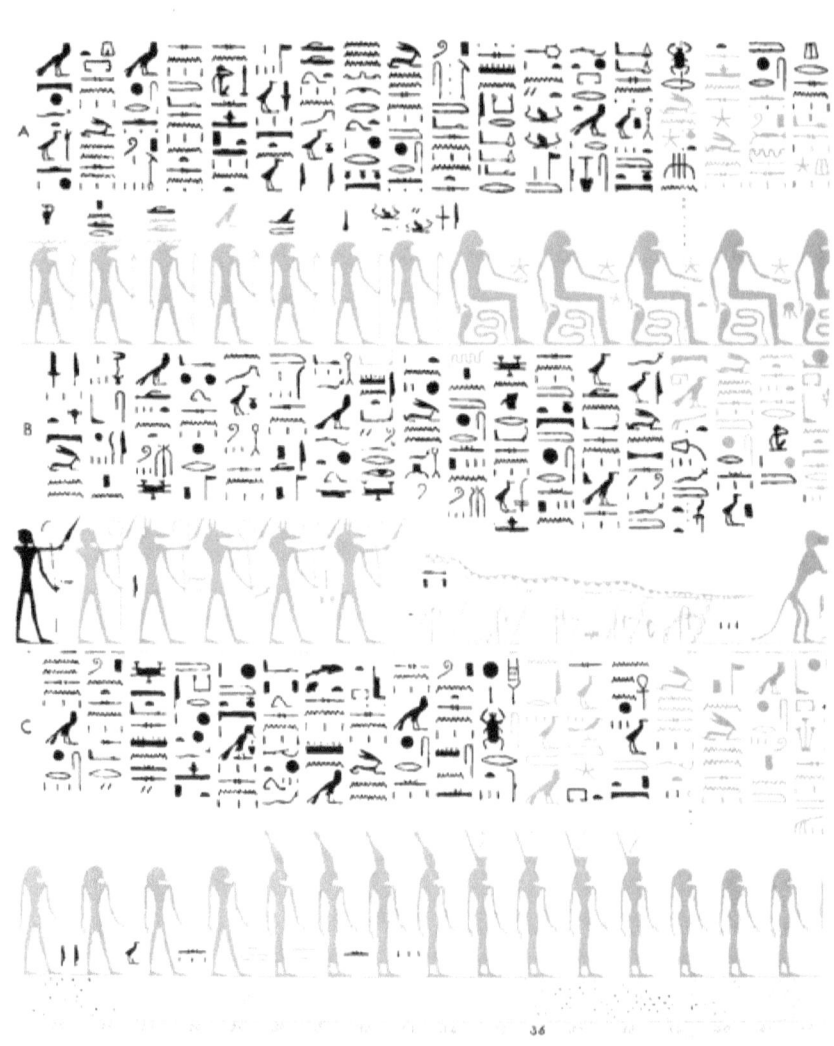

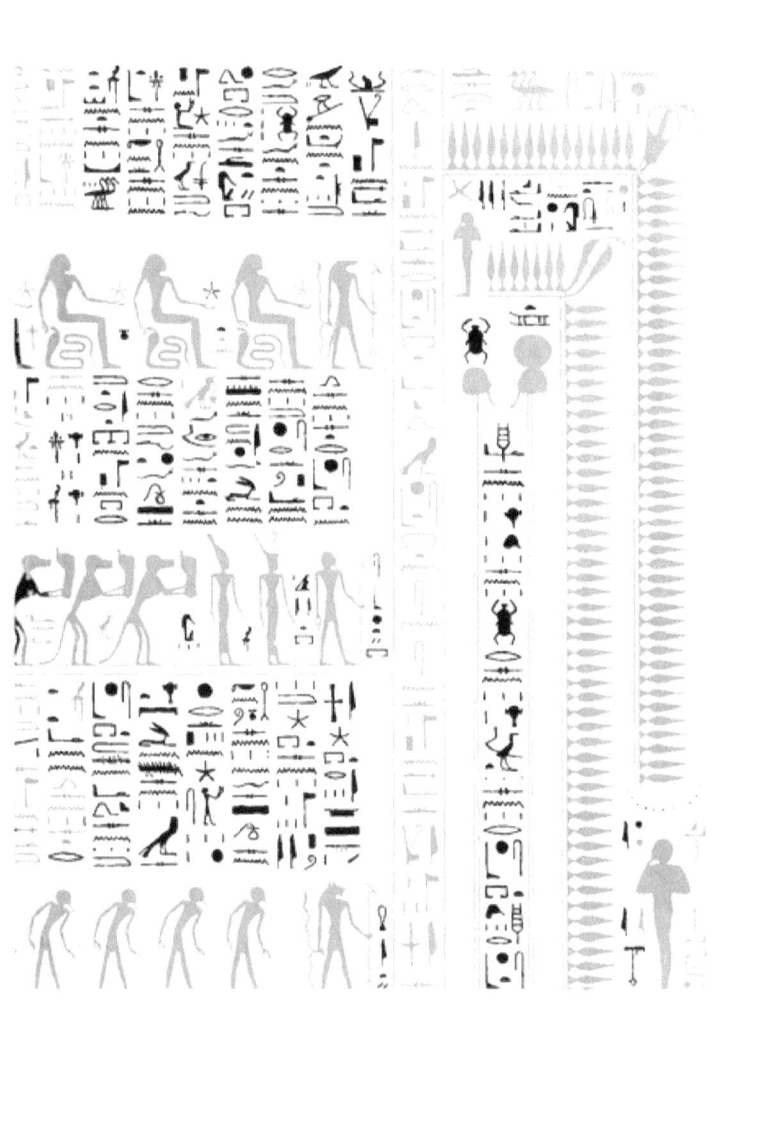

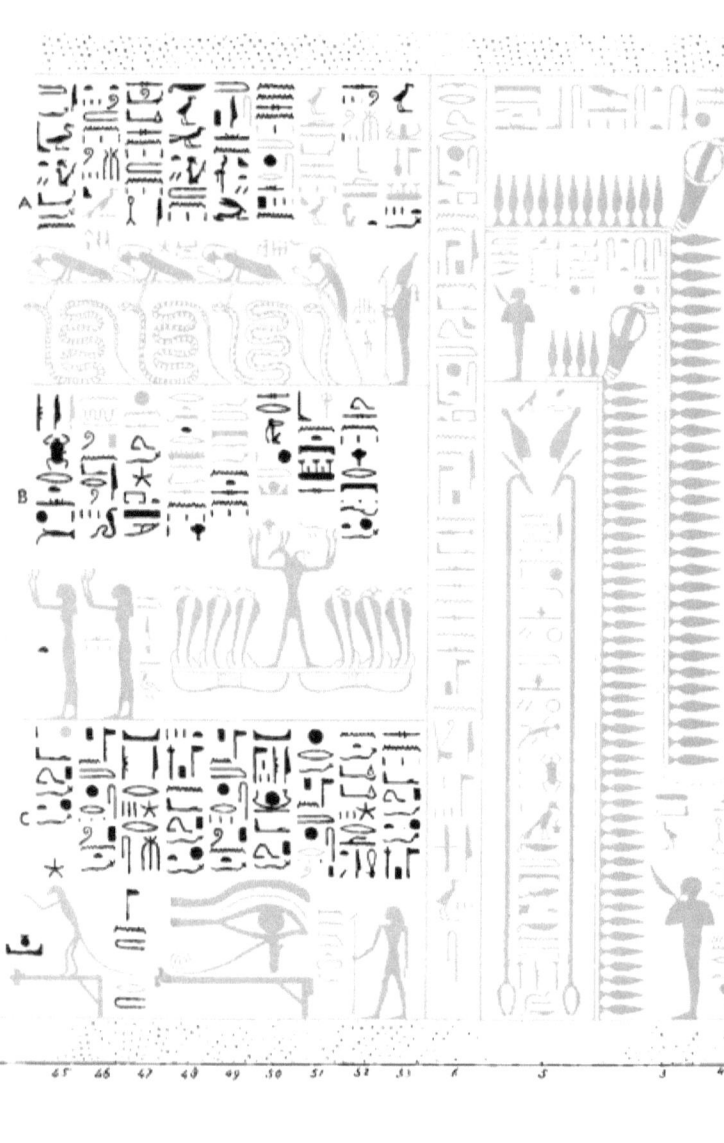

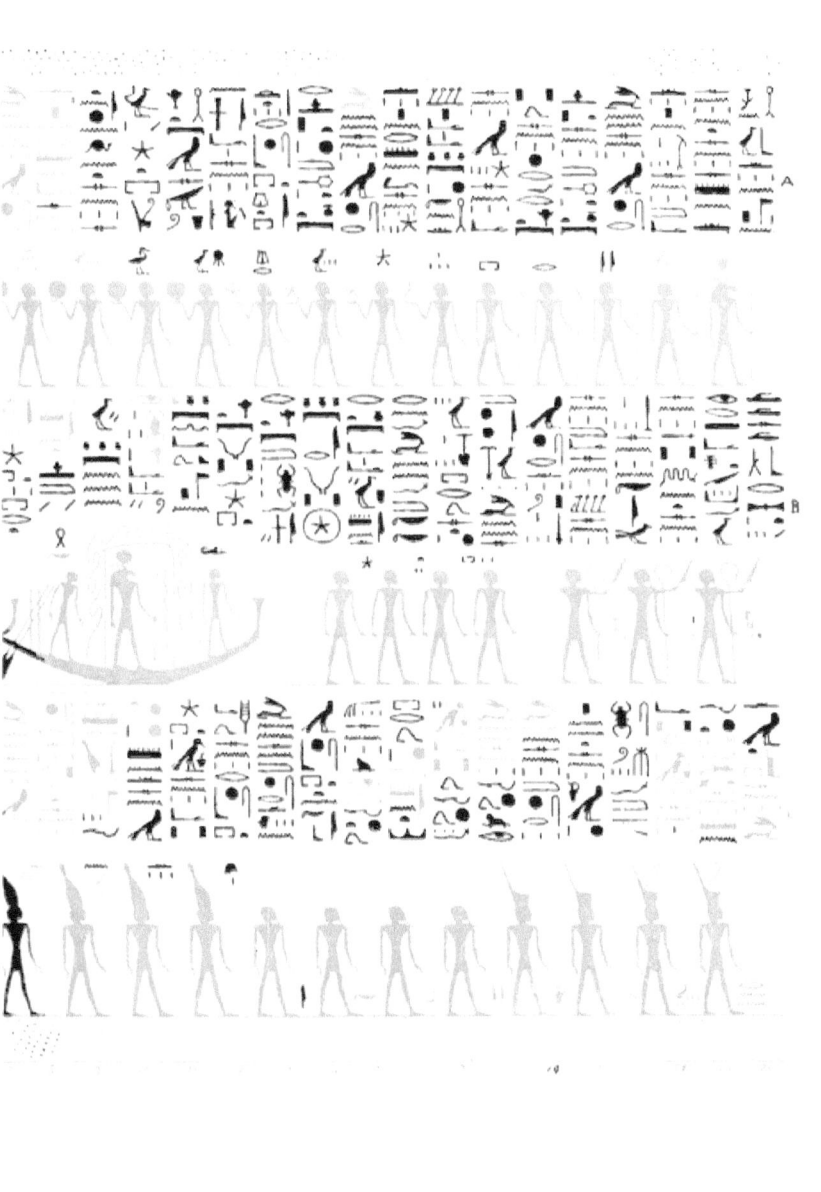

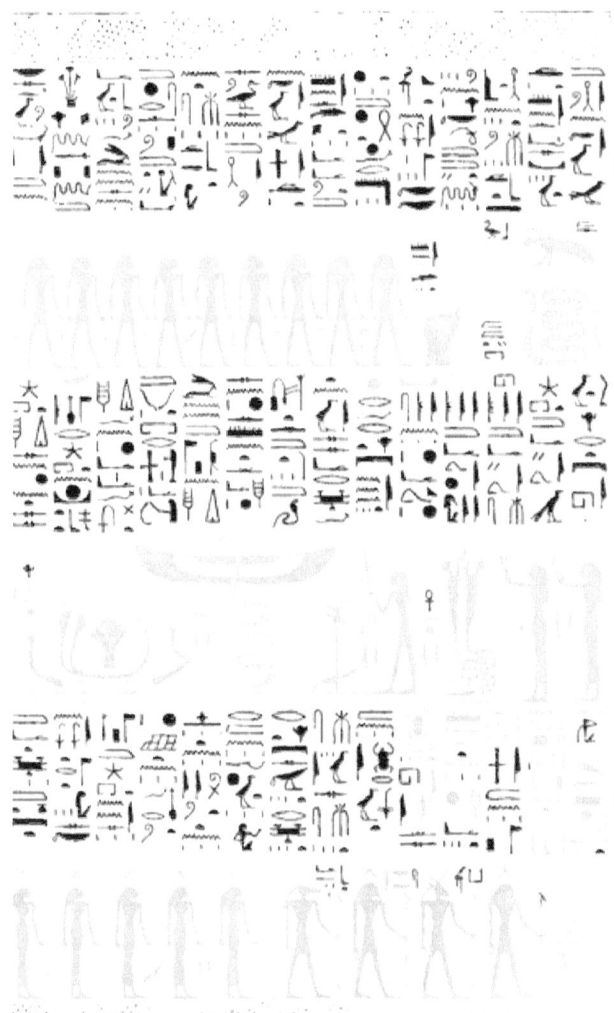

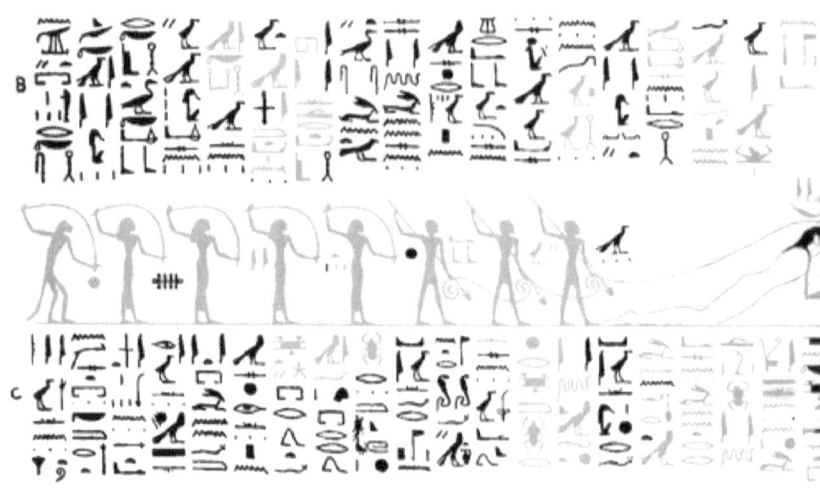

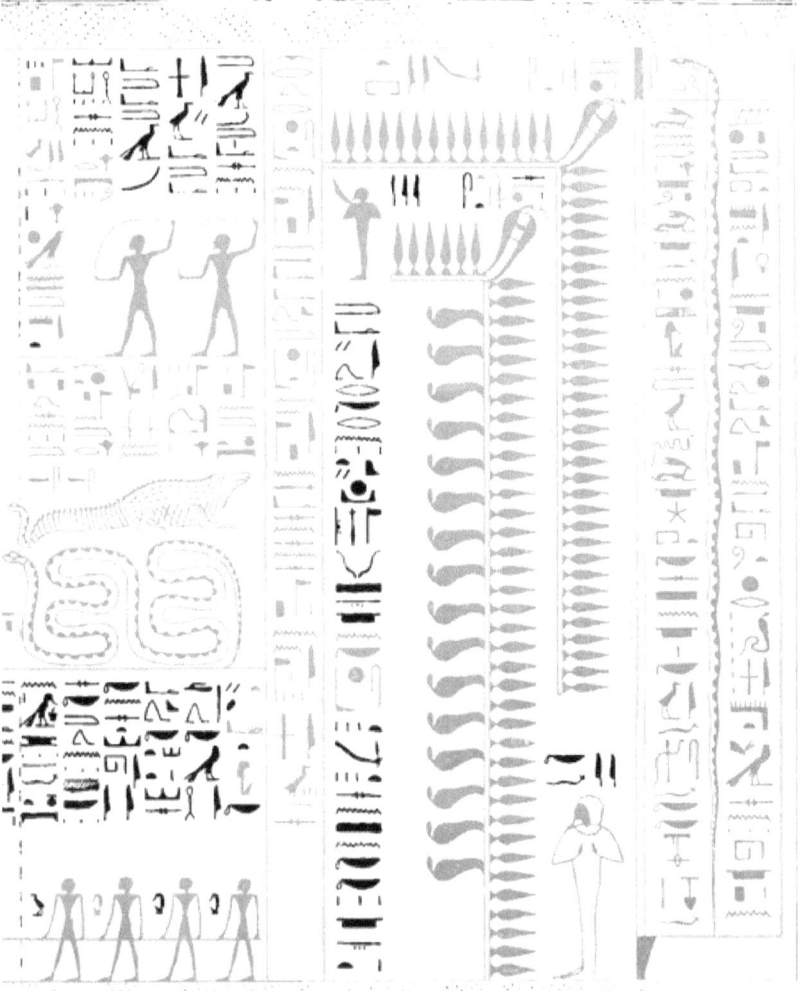

PLATE 12

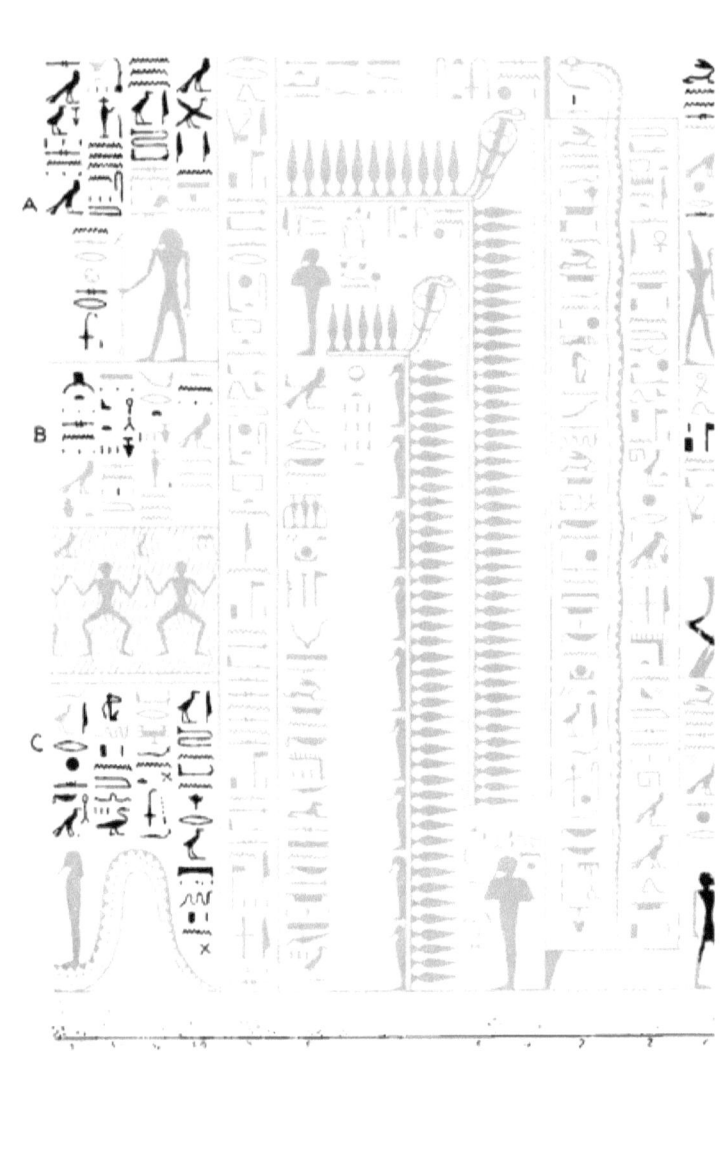

PLATE 13

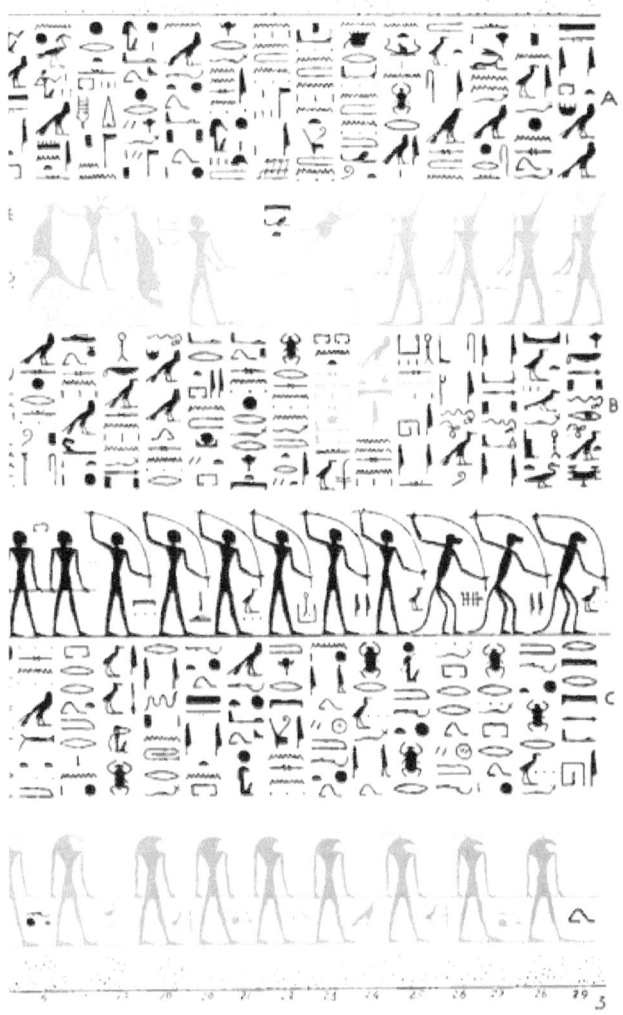

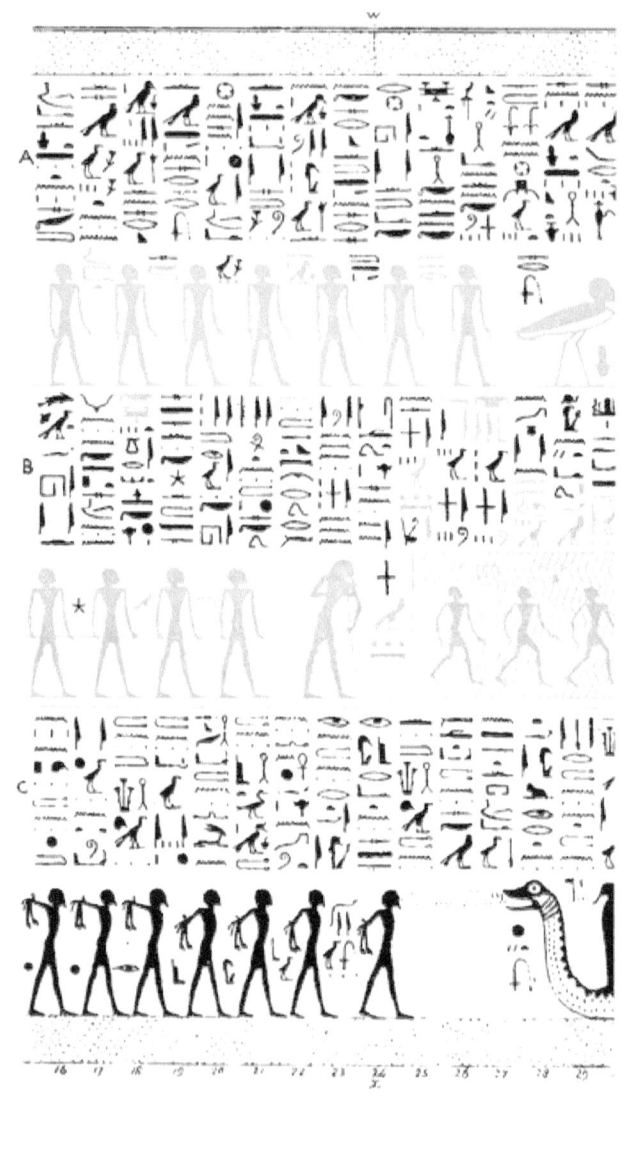

PLATE 14

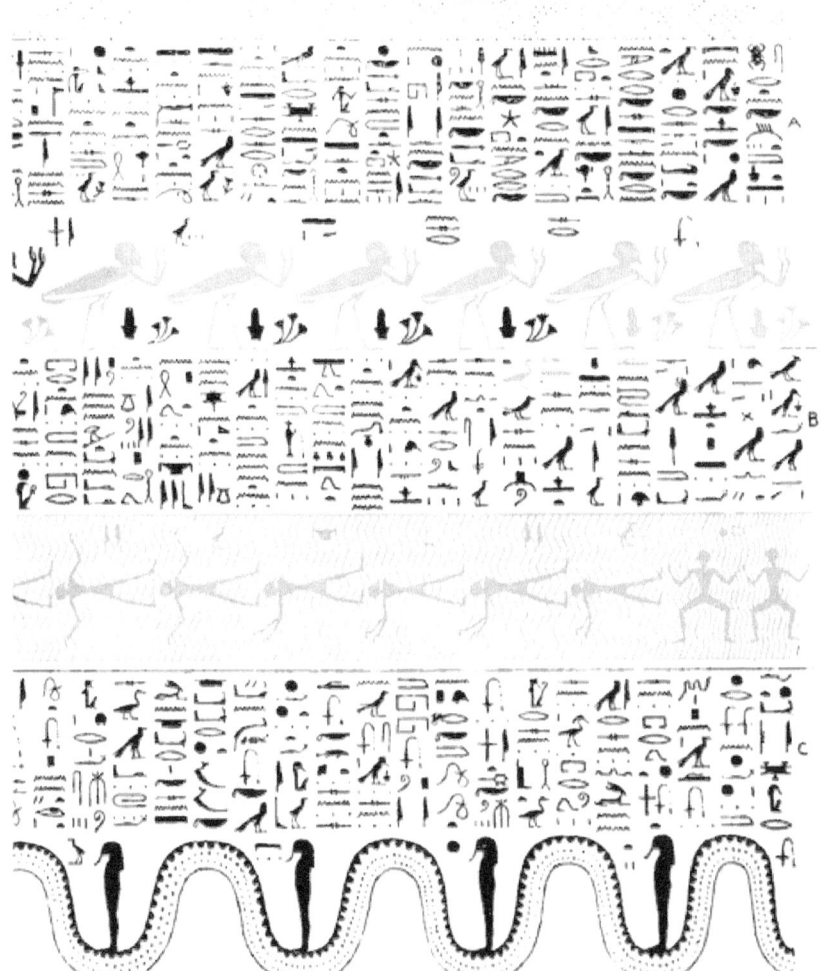

PLATE 15

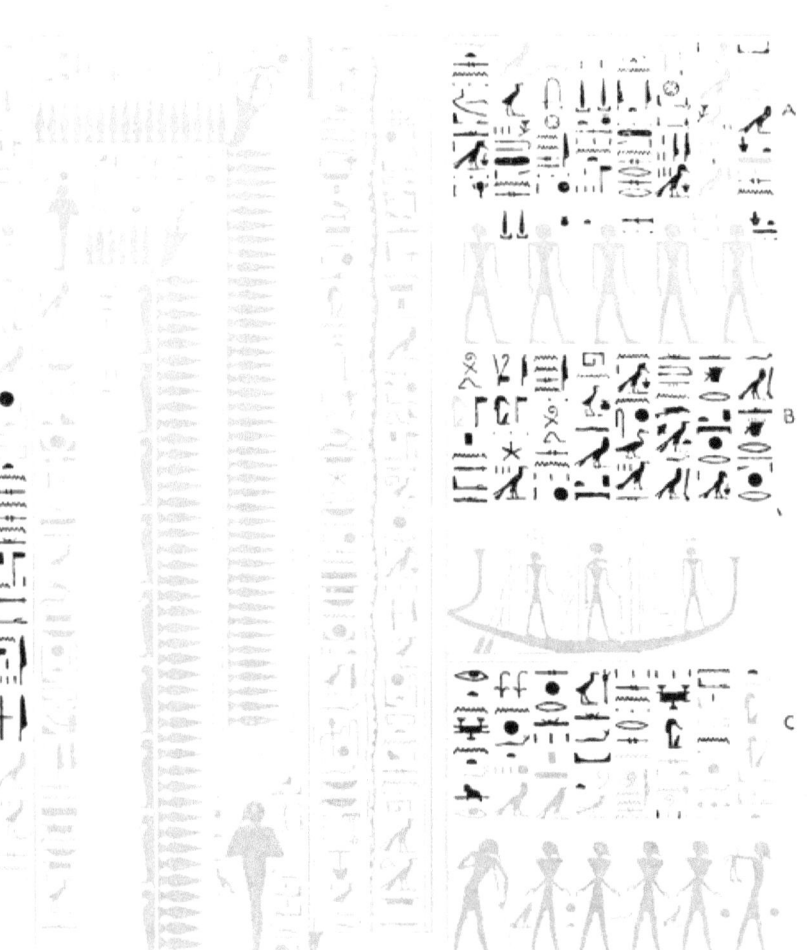

PLATE 16

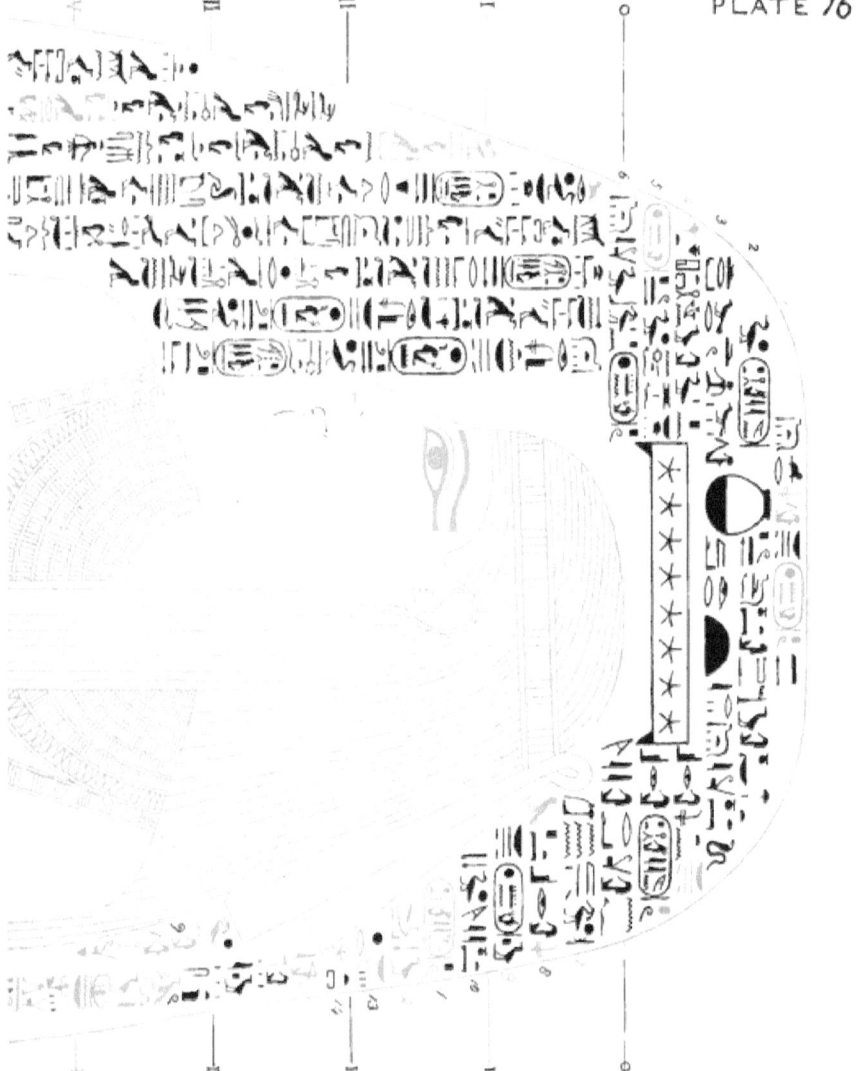

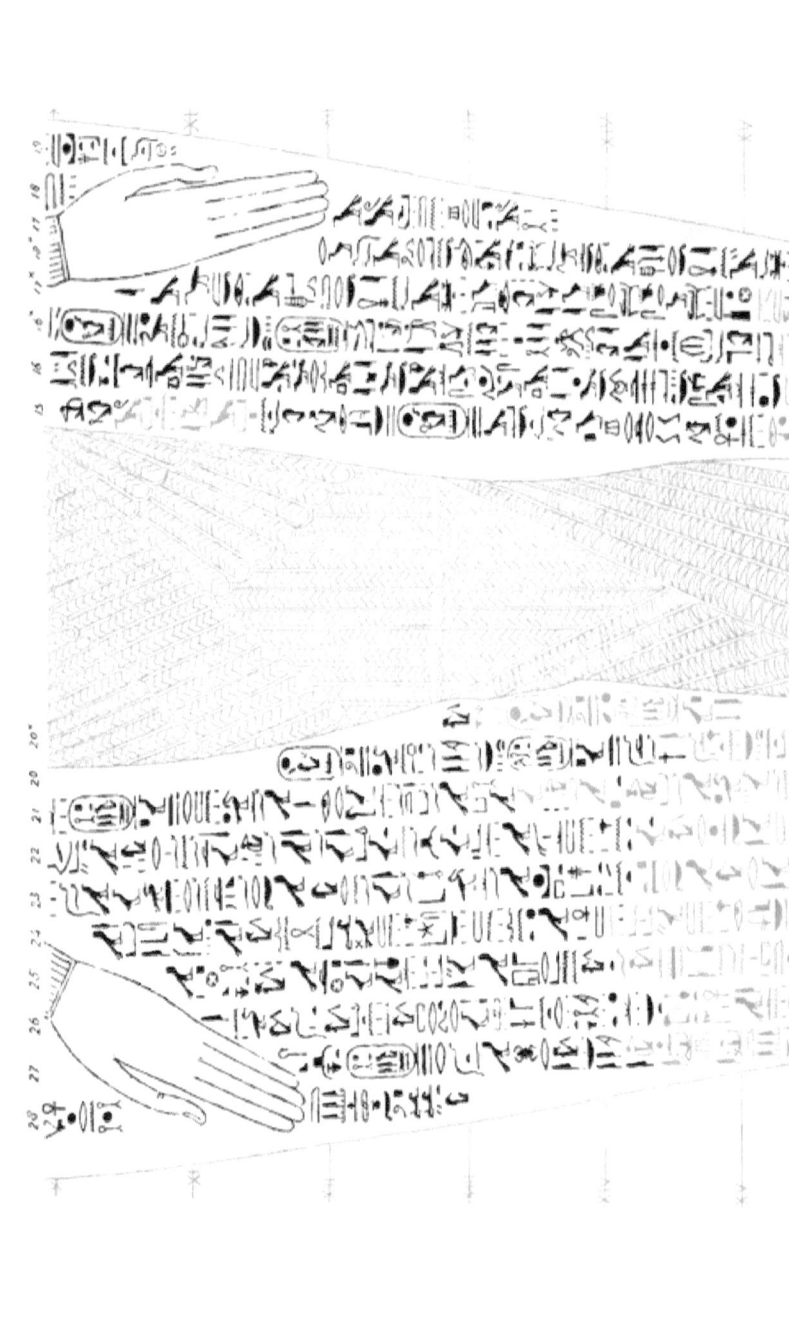

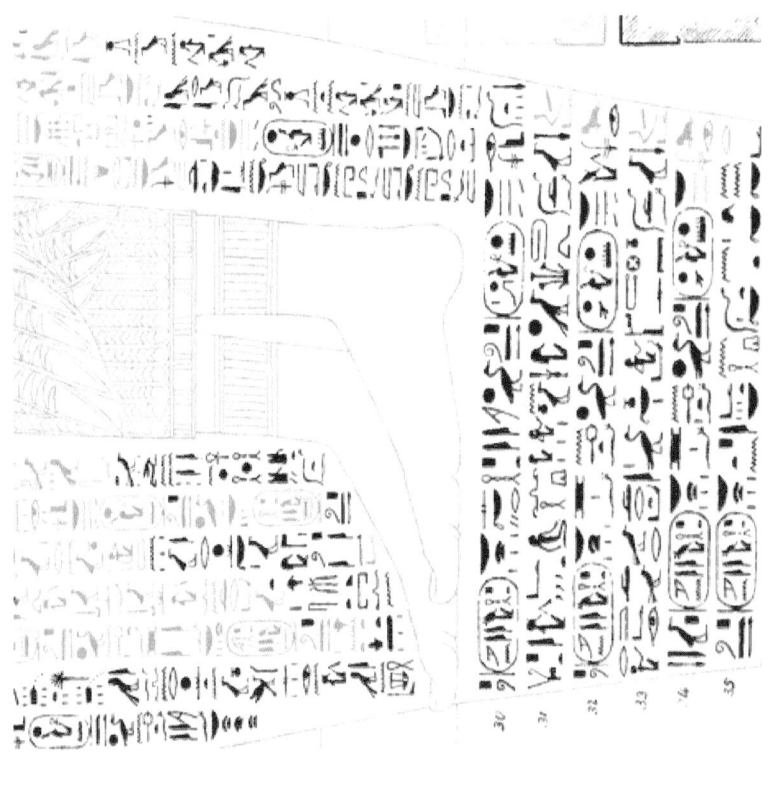

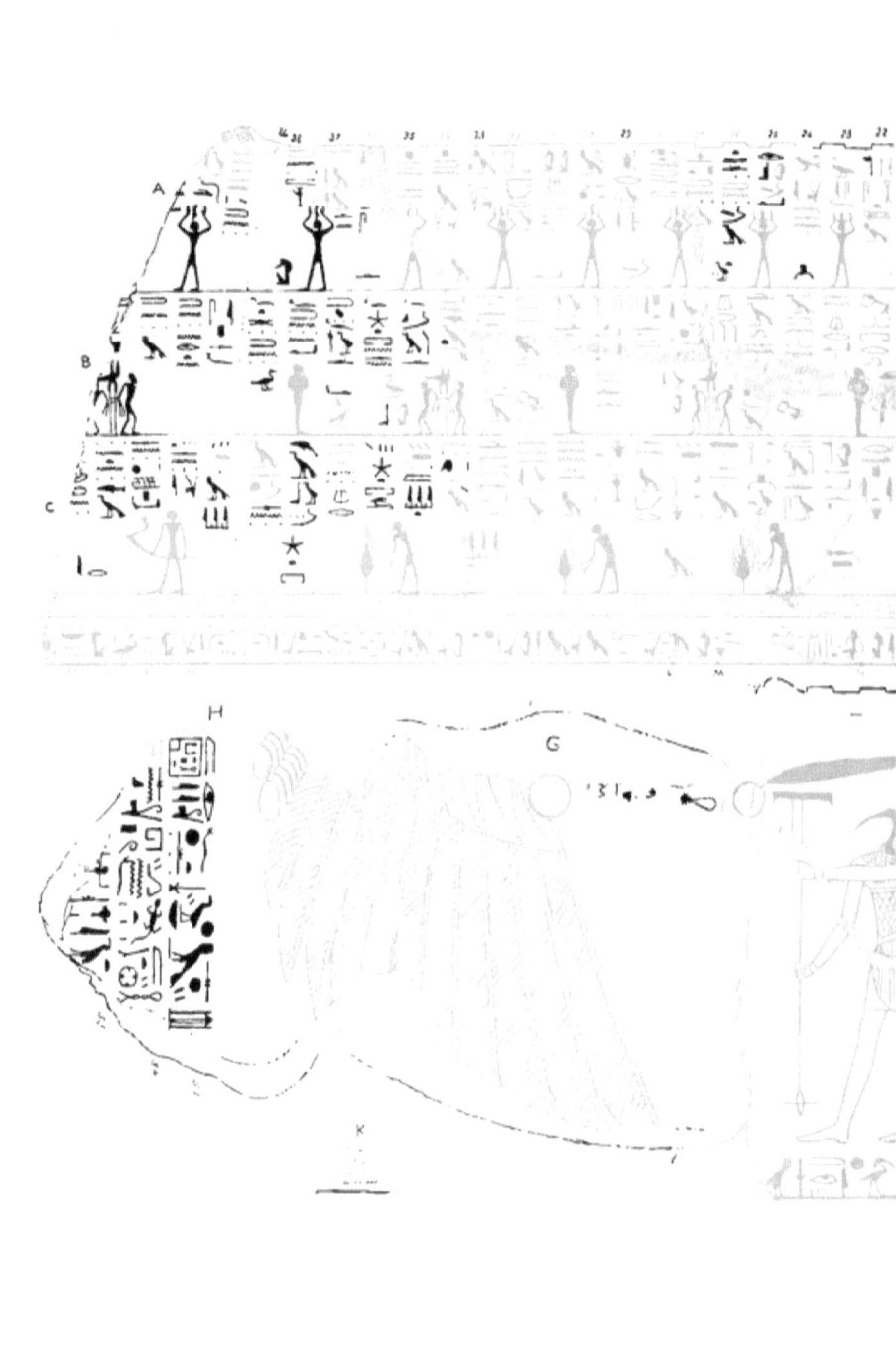

PLATE 18

PLATE 19

www.ingramcontent.com/pod-product-compliance
Lightning Source LLC
Chambersburg PA
CBHW021940160426
43195CB00011B/1165